The Five-Minute Solution

"Dost thou love life? Then do not squander time, for that's the stuff life is made of."

—Benjamin Franklin
American statesman (1706–90)

The Five-Minute Solution

Hundreds of Smart Ideas to Make Spare Minutes Work Harder for You

Mary Frances Budzik

Reader's
Digest

The Reader's Digest Association, Inc.
Pleasantville, New York

A READER'S DIGEST BOOK

This edition published by The Reader's Digest Association, Inc.
by arrangement with Toucan Books Ltd.

Copyright © 2009 Toucan Books Ltd.

FOR READER'S DIGEST
U.S. Project Editor Kim Casey
Cover/Project Designer Jennifer Tokarski
Senior Art Director George McKeon
Executive Editor, Trade Publishing Dolores York
Associate Publisher Rosanne McManus
President and Publisher, Trade Publishing Harold Clarke

Library of Congress Cataloging-in-Publication Data
Budzik, Mary Frances, 1955-
The five-minute solution : hundreds of smart ideas to make
spare minutes work harder for you / Mary Frances Budzik.
p. cm.
ISBN 978-1-60652-038-3
1. Time management. 2. Self-management (Psychology) I. Title.
BF637.T5.B83 2009
640' .43--dc22   2009018612

We are committed to both the quality of our products and the
service we provide to our customers. We value your comments,
so please feel free to contact us.

The Reader's Digest Association, Inc.
Adult Trade Publishing
Reader's Digest Road
Pleasantville, NY 10570-7000

For more Reader's Digest products and information, visit our website:
www.rd.com (in the United States)

NOTE TO OUR READERS
The health-related information in this book should not be substituted
for, or used to alter, medical therapy without your doctor's advice.
For a specific health problem, consult your physician for guidance.

The instructions for the do-it-yourself ideas in this publication have been rigorously checked for
accuracy. Please review all instructions carefully before undertaking any project.

Printed in Singapore
1 3 5 7 9 10 8 6 4 2

Contents

INTRODUCTION

This book is about opening up the possibilities of those throwaway segments of time that everyday life imposes on us. It's an oddity of modernity that despite the speediness of practically every task we undertake— from doing the laundry (no more washboards or handwringers) to sending a message across oceans (if it takes more than a few minutes, we get impatient)—we never seem to have any time. No time, that is, except for all those minutes spent staring into space or gritting our teeth as we listen to the prerecorded cheer of a canned message while on hold, stand in a motor-vehicle department line that moves at a pitilessly torpid pace, or sit at a loss at home for vacant minutes as we wait for a call to come in, a ride to arrive, or a package to be delivered.

It's our lack of control over these waits that makes them so stressful. However, *The Five-Minute Solution* is here to help you gain the upper hand, full of suggestions to help you change your perspective and transform the desert of waiting time into an oasis of opportunity for productivity or even pleasure.

Solutions for Different Situations

Here you'll find short, succinct tasks to help you take charge of those irksome intervals and transform them from drab to doable. The book's six chapters track down wasted time where it is most likely to lurk—in a winding bank line, while listening to an impenetrable, prerecorded phone answering system, a parking lot—yes, even in your own home—and provide you with a multitude of tasks to turn aside the tedium. You'll find some of these five-minute solutions are true multitaskers that can work in more than one situation, so don't restrict yourself by where they appear in the book—though you do need to keep in mind the circumstances around you. You can improve your vocal technique either at home or in the car, for example, but it would be inadvisable to implement this particular boredom buster deep within a maze of densely packed, corporate cubicles.

Hundreds of Suggestions

Each chapter offers a variety of solutions, from the practical to the pleasurable. You'll find suggestions to help you become more organized, homemaking and crafts techniques, step-by-step exercises, advice to keep you healthy, ideas for self-education, and even ways to pamper yourself. Whether you want to be up-to-date with technology by learning to text message like a teenager or prefer to follow an old-fashioned recipe for a soothing foot soak, you can live your five minutes to the hilt.

You'll have a sense of accomplishment at the end of your wait—in fact, it might even seem like the time was too short! Compose your own personal motto as you stand in line or wait in traffic, learn to dance a waltz even if your only partner happens to be a telephone receiver, scan the sky to identify bird flight patterns high above as you enjoy the outdoors, or memorize a few choice words in Urdu or Croatian while in the comfort of your own home. Whatever you choose, you're certain to be inspired by variety, not vapidity, in just five minutes.

CHAPTER ONE

On Hold

There's something about being on hold while on the telephone that brings out the impatient side in each of us. However, if you can accomplish something interesting while maintaining a calm demeanor, you will feel more satisfied. In this chapter, you'll find a few diversions to smooth your path toward Zen while listening to elevator music.

A Pain in the Neck

If you have a cordless phone, it gives you the freedom to perform other activities while you carry on with your conversation. However, many people tuck the phone in between a shoulder and an ear—usually the same one each time (this is also true when using an older phone with a cord).

Over time this posture can cause stress to the joints in your cervical spine (neck), shoulder, and scapular (shoulder blade) as it compresses them. The associated muscle groups can also be shortened, which can lead to tightness and muscle imbalance. These symptoms may not be obvious at first, but can build up with repeated use, resulting in headaches, neck pain, and arm or shoulder pain. Prevention is the key:

- Hold the receiver to your ear.

- If your phone has a speaker option, take a few minutes to learn how to use it before making a call in which you expect to be placed on hold for awhile.

- If you must have your hands free and do not have a speaker phone, use the ear-shoulder side that you least favor, thereby encouraging you to use it as little possible.

. . . .

CALL CENTER KARAOKE

Instead of gritting your teeth and feeling your blood pressure rise with yet another chorus of "Song Sung Blue," "Chariots of Fire," the "Miami Vice Theme," or another call center favorite, go with the flow and sing along. Even if you don't like the song, you might know the words by heart. What better time is there to make the song more interesting by changing some of the words? However, unless you're an extrovert or a trained singer, you'll probably prefer to do this when no one else is in earshot.

Q: Why do call centers play music to people put on hold?

A: According to one survey, 36 percent of the respondents said they hated listening to music while on hold. Yet, on average, people hang on for 20 percent longer if they listen to music than if there is only silence.

....

Bravo Charlie!

If you have an unusual name, you know what it's like to spell it out over the phone and still be misunderstood—sometimes with unfortunate consequences, such as misdirected mail or being registered for an event or subscription under the wrong name. The pilot's alphabet, also known as the NATO phonetic alphabet, can solve your problem. It was developed during the early days of aviation radio communication, when noisy cockpits made it difficult for pilots to transmit crucial messages.

The pilot's alphabet is still commonly used today in the military and by police and emergency dispatchers, and it is widely understood. The quirky, colorful nature of the alphabet makes it easy to remember. The next time you are trying to spell something over the phone, don't say "Z, not B!," say "Z as in Zulu!" Here is the alphabet to memorize:

A = Alpha	**J** = Juliet	**S** = Sierra
B = Bravo	**K** = Kilo	**T** = Tango
C = Charlie	**L** = Lima	**U** = Uniform
D = Delta	**M** = Mike	**V** = Victor
E = Echo	**N** = November	**W** = Whiskey
F = Foxtrot	**O** = Oscar	**X** = X-ray
G = Golf	**P** = Papa	**Y** = Yankee
H = Hotel	**Q** = Quebec	**Z** = Zulu
I = India	**R** = Romeo	

Cut to the Chase

Please Don't Go

In the lingo of the "On Hold" industry, when a caller hangs up it is commonly referred to as "caller abandonment."

You may not need this section if you're near a computer and do an Internet search for "bypass phone." You'll find updated databases that list the secrets for bypassing the recorded answering systems to reach a real live person. These vary depending on the company, but here are some tips:

1. Just simply stay on hold, pretending that you have only an old-fashioned rotary phone.

2. Interrupt. Press 0 (or 0# or #0 or 0* or *0) repeatedly, sometimes quickly (the same keystroke does not work for every company). Many interactive voice response (IVR) systems will connect to a human after a few "invalid entries," although some IVRs will disconnect the call.

3. Talk. Say "get human" (or "representative" or "agent"), or raise your voice, or mumble. The IVR might connect you to a human after one of these key or unknown phrases.

4. Connect to accounts receivable or sales or account cancellation; they always seem to answer quickly. First ask the employee for his or her name and employee number (so the employee knows you are writing it down, and will be more likely to help you.) Then ask to be transferred to the department you need. Sometimes you will be put ahead of the line, although sometimes you will be sent to the end.

5. If the expected wait time is too long for credit card calls made to a toll-free number, hang up and try to call back on their standard business number, which will often have shorter lines.

6. Select the option for Spanish. This will sometimes get you a bilingual human more quickly than if you just waited for an English-only operator.

What's That You Say?

To add to your annoyance while you're on hold, are you straining to hear the recording? It may be time to review the following questions to assess your hearing. If you answer yes to more than two of these questions, make an appointment with an audiologist for a formal hearing test. Hearing loss is a common disability, affecting at least 28 million Americans of all ages.

- Do you have a problem hearing over the telephone?
- Do you hear better with one ear than the other when you are on the telephone?
- Do you have trouble following the conversation when two or more people are talking at the same time?
- Do people complain that you turn the television volume up too high?
- Do you have to strain to understand conversation?
- Do you have trouble hearing when there is noise in the background?
- Do you have trouble hearing in restaurants?
- Do you have dizziness, pain, or ringing in your ears?
- Do you frequently ask people to repeat themselves?
- Do family members or coworkers remark that you are missing what has been said?
- Do many people you talk to seem to be mumbling?
- Do you sometimes misunderstand what others are saying and respond inappropriately?
- Do you have trouble understanding the speech of women and children?

For more information on having your hearing tested by an ASHA certified audiologist, contact:

The American Speech-Language-Hearing Association
2200 Research Boulevard
Rockville, MD 20850–3289
1-800-638–8255

GATHER YOUR **EVIDENCE**

If you are calling a company to complain about a bill or service, frustration may take over by the time your call is answered and you can forget to mention important details. It's a good idea to outline the points you want to make and the specifics of your complaint. Remember to note dates, account and check numbers, and other pertinent facts, so that you don't forget anything when you reach a customer service agent. Of course, it is better to do this before making the call—just in case you're not put on hold!

. . . .

Get Yourself Out of a Verbal Rut

Building up your vocabulary can come in handy when talking to a customer service operator who is not being helpful. If you're near a copy of *Roget's Thesaurus,* look through it and make a list of synonyms for words you overuse. For example, do you overdo "actually"? You'll think twice when you scan this list of its synonyms and ask yourself what you are...actually...trying to express. Is it:

admittedly, assuredly, believingly, beyond question, certainly, clearly, decidedly, demonstrably, devoutly, doubtless, doubtlessly, for a certainty, for real, in all conscience, incontestably, indeed, indisputably, indubitably, irrefragably, irrefutably, manifestly, no doubt, noticeably, observably, obviously, on faith, on trust, out of the question, patently, piously, positively, quite, really, sensibly, seriously, truly, trustfully, trustingly, unambigously, undeniably, undoubtedly, undoubtfully, undoubtingly, unmistakably, unquestionably, unquestioningly, unsuspectingly, unsuspiciously, upon trust, verily, visibly, with confidence, with faith, without doubt...?

What's in a Name?

The word "thesaurus" dates from 1736 and means "treasury or store of knowledge." Peter Roget (1779–1869), an English physician who compiled the first thesaurus, was obsessed with making lists.

Q: Are all toll-free calls free?

A: No, not if they are made from a cell phone, with the exception of an emergency call. Unless it's an emergency, save your calls to 1-800 number phone calls for a landline telephone—particularly if there is a high risk that you will be placed on hold for a long time!

BALANCE YOUR CHECKBOOK

You may not be able to do a full-fledged reconciliation of your records with the bank's in the time you're on hold. However, if you have just your checkbook handy, you can add up your outstanding checks and debits and compare them to your deposits and your best estimate of your current balance. And don't forget to factor in any bank fees in the debit column and earned interest in the credit column. Keeping an up-to-date idea of your available cash is the best way to avoid costly and embarrassing check bounces.

Improve Your Handwriting

Has your handwriting turned into a sloppy scrawl? Why not learn to write in old-fashioned italics? Choose a font that you like from a word-processing program, and print out the entire alphabet in that font. Practice writing sentences on lined paper, using as many letters as possible from the font. Here's one sentence used to practice typing that has all the letters in the alphabet:

> The quick brown fox jumps over the lazy dog.

"Life is not so short but that there is always time for courtesy."
—Ralph Waldo Emerson
American writer (1803–82)

Release Your Inner Fashionista

Sketch a design for a hat, pair of shoes, jacket, or pair of earrings. Plan the color, material, tailoring, and style. Cost is no object—unless you follow up on your plans!

. . . .

SKETCH A **STILL LIFE**

Making Plans

Now is a good time to sketch out the plan of a garden, a room rearrangement, or of an embroidery that you'd like to do.

Wherever you are and whatever objects surround you, there's ample material for a still life. You've got five minutes, maybe a red or blue pen, a pencil, or if you're lucky some colored pencils. Look around, choose an object you see every day or maybe a small collection of objects—your coffee cup, the pottery jar that holds your pens, your computer mouse, your upturned eyeglasses— and sketch them. It doesn't have to be worthy of hanging in a gallery. Date your sketch, and write the time of day and maybe a particular fact about the minutes in time that you made the sketch in a little legend below the drawing. You'll be surprised how poignant and telling this vignette will become in later years if you save it in a scrapbook or journal. Sketching is also therapeutic. A 2004 study published in the *Journal of Nursing Scholarship* found that creating artwork and doing crafts relaxed a group of adults who were serving as caregivers for family members with cancer.

. . . .

PRIMP YOUR **PLANT'S PORES**

With the phone in speaker mode, take a plant into the bathroom or kitchen and wash off its leaves gently with a damp paper towel. And don't forget the bottom of the leaves! Plants breathe through stomata, or microscopic pores, on the undersides of the leaves. A gentle wipe ensures that your plant will not be trying to catch a breath through dust-clogged stomata. You can trim any scraggly leaves or trailing growth at the same time, using a pair of scissors. Never tug the leaves out—you might end up removing healthy growth, too.

Make a Tangram

Tangrams, Chinese for "seven boards of skill," were first brought to the West as presents for children by sailors returning from Asia. The seven "boards" were put in different arrangements to create shapes and pictures. Tangram puzzles were made from precious materials, such as ivory, but it's easy to make one from paper or cardboard. Playing with a tangram will develop your ability to solve spatial and geometry problems. The writer Lewis Carroll and French emperor Napoleon Bonaparte were both devotees. Here's how to make one:

1. Make a square by folding over the corner of an 8½ x 11-inch (21 x 28-cm) sheet of paper to the other side of the paper, so that it aligns with the edge. There will be a rectangle at the top of the paper. Cut that off, then unfold.

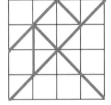

2. Fold the square in half four times: twice lengthwise and twice widthwise. Unfold. The paper will be marked by the folds into 16 even squares.

3. Mark the pattern above on the paper, using the 16 even squares as a guide, and cut apart along the marked lines. Voilà, you have the seven puzzle pieces of the tangram.

4. Test your ability to arrange them in traditional shapes, such as the duck or candle shown at right. Do not let the pieces overlap.

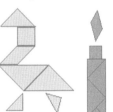

Stitch Your Life Back Together

If you know that you're likely to be put on hold when making a call, take five minutes to gather a needle, thread, and your other sewing paraphernalia and mend some of the frayed seams in your life. You can:

- Fix that pocket hole that is responsible for the loss of your coffee money last week.

- Give your child's teddy bear the gift of sight by restoring its button eye.

- Restore the fluffy cotton intestines of a disemboweled stuffed animal and sew up the split seam.

- Sew a button on your favorite shirt or coat so that you don't have to leave it "casually" unbuttoned despite frigid temperatures.

- Repair the hem of that skirt that you fixed with the office stapler (and it has been that way since last season).

Cuddle Up

Turn your on-hold captivity into a moment of family peace. Call over one of your children for a snuggle, or a hairbrushing session.

....

REINCARNATE YOUR **SWEATER**

If you have a beautiful old wool sweater that's past its prime, you can unravel the yarn while you're sitting idle on hold and wind the yarn into a ball. Cut out worn spots and simply retie the yarn to the next good length. You can use the recycled yarn to knit a scarf, a hat, a child's toy, or use it for children's craft projects.

....

FIX YOUR **WOBBLY FURNITURE**

If you have a bookshelf, cabinet, futon frame, or other furniture that you proudly assembled yourself, it may be showing the loosey-goosey evidence of the fasteners working their way free. Look for the Allen wrench or screwdriver that you used to first assemble the piece, then spend a few minutes tightening the fittings and fasteners while you are waiting on hold. This will be easier to do, of course, if you use a phone with a speaker option.

Can You Still Name the Actor?

Sweeten your temper while you're on hold by indulging in some fond memories of the television sitcom in its heyday—the 1960s and 70s. Test your memory at the same time by trying to name some of the stars you once knew so well. Who played:

1. Murray, the sardonic newswriter, in *The Mary Tyler Moore Show* (1970–77)?

2. Potsie, Richie Cunningham's closest friend, in *Happy Days* (1974–84)?

3. Edith, "dingbat" wife of the insufferable Archie Bunker, in *All in the Family* (1971–79)?

4. Donald Hollinger, Ann's protective journalist boyfriend, in *That Girl* (1966–71)?

5. Julie, the gorgeous, laid-back police officer, in *The Mod Squad* (1968–73)?

6. The Professor, the nerdy castaway scientist, in *Gilligan's Island* (1964–67)?

7. Vinnie Barbarino, the cool, "unofficial, official" leader of the Sweathogs, in *Welcome Back, Kotter* (1975–79)?

8. Endora, the imperious witch and scathing mother-in-law, in *Bewitched* (1964–69)?

9. Bobby, the freckled-speckled and youngest Brady male, in *The Brady Bunch* (1969–74)?

10. Laurie, the beautiful rock starlet/keyboard player and sister to David Cassidy, in *The Partridge Family* (1970–74)?

. . . .

ANSWERS

1. Gavin McLeod (later "The Captain" on *The Love Boat*); 2. Anson Williams; 3. Jean Stapleton; 4. Ted Bessell; 5. Peggy Lipton; 6. Russell Johnson; 7. John Travolta; 8. Agnes Moorehead; 9. Mike Lookinland; 10. Susan Dey

FINE-TUNE YOUR **CHOPSTICKS** SKILLS

Learn to dine gracefully in the Asian manner and improve your dexterity by practicing how to eat with chopsticks. Start by curling your pinkie, ring, and middle fingers; they will form a steady base for the bottom chopstick. Rest the bottom chopstick in the notch between thumb and index finger and on the base. The bottom chopstick needs to remain stationary to serve as a pivot for the top chopstick. It is grasped like a pencil, between your thumb and index finger, and it is manipulated by them to grasp a piece of food. The ends of the chopsticks need to be even without crossing, and the tips will be parallel. For beginners, it is easier to hold both chopsticks toward the end of the stick.

Chopsticks Etiquette

To avoid embarrassment, keep in mind these basic rules of chopstick etiquette if you are dining in an Asian country:

- Do not resort to a frustrated stab—spearing food with a chopstick is considered rude.

- Do not wave chopsticks or point with them.

- Put chopsticks down by laying them in front of you with the tips to the left. If there is a chopsticks stand, use it.

- It's acceptable to pick up a large piece of food with chopsticks and take a bite from it.

- Use the opposite end of the chopsticks to take food from a common dish.

- Do not stick chopsticks upright into any food, particularly rice. During Japanese funerals, chopsticks are stuck upright into a bowl of rice and placed on the altar.

The Foreign Diplomat

If you are feeling like you are being held prisoner by your phone line, you may have the urge to run away to foreign climes. If you do, be sure you don't cause any international incidents. The OK sign of the index finger and thumb together used in this country, for example, is considered obscene in Brazil, rude in Greece and Russia, means zero in France, and refers to money in Japan. You also might want to avoid these foreign faux pas:

- **Cambodia and Thailand** Never touch, pat, or pass something over a Cambodian's head, which is sacred.

- **China** Slapping a back or putting an arm around an acquaintance's shoulder is considered too forward.

- **Colombia** Yawning is definitely out of the question.

- **Egypt** Sitting with your legs crossed is insulting.

- **Finland** It's arrogant to fold your arms while talking and gauche to cross your legs at the ankles.

- **Greece** A slight upward nod of the head means yes; tilting the head to one side, then the other, no.

- **India** No leather shoes, handbags, or belts as gifts! The Hindus hold the cow sacred.

- **Japan** Unless a family member or close friend, never address a Japanese person by his or her first name.

- **Korea** If you laugh, cover your mouth—something that the Koreans do when they laugh.

- **Malaysia and Muslim countries** Do not eat or pass food with your left hand, because it is considered unclean.

- **Muslim countries** Never expose the soles of your feet. They are considered the dirtiest parts of the body.

- **Paraguay** Don't cross your fingers—this is an offensive gesture.

- **Philippines** Watch your words when you're visiting. "Hostess" translates to "prostitute" in Tagalog.

- **Taiwan** Blinking your eyes at someone is rude.

Ancient Names

If you're a bit bored while on hold, what better time for a little self-education? You can improve your knowledge of classic history by memorizing the names of the Titan or Olympian Greek gods and goddesses. What's the difference? The Greek gods were all family—the Olympians were descended from the Titans—however, power struggles and strife, not love, ruled their lineage.

The oldest Greek Gods were the Titans, the elemental deities born to Gaia, Mother Earth, through her mating with her self-generated son, Uranus, the sky god. Uranus' rule ended when he was castrated by Cronus, his son with Gaia (making Gaia both his mother and grandmother). Cronus tried to prevent a similar fate by eating all of his children, but he was finally tricked by his wife, Rhea, into swallowing a stone instead of his son Zeus.

Zeus overthrew his father Cronus and became the ruler and father of the 12 Olympians. This was the new generation of gods named for their home, Mount Olympus, where they sparred with each other and meddled in the affairs of mortal men. The Titans were closely identified with the creative and destructive powers of the cosmos; the younger Olympians had more human characteristics—usually lust and jealousy—that got them into trouble.

Titans	Olympians
Coeus	Aphrodite
Crius	Apollo
Cronus	Ares
Hyperion	Artemis
Iapetus	Athena
Mnemosyne	Demeter
Oceanus	Hades
Phoebe	Hephaestus
Rhea	Hera
Tethys	Hermes
Thea	Poseidon
Themis	Zeus

Seven Wonders of the Ancient World

Idioms from the seven ancient wonders are sometimes heard today; for example, the Hanging Gardens of Babylon are used to describe something that is decadently opulent. Use your time on hold to learn about these seven wonders, compiled by the Greek writer Herodotus (484–425 B.C.):

- **Great Pyramid of Giza** Built as the tomb of Egyptian pharaoh Khufu in 2584–2561 B.C., it is still standing.

- **Hanging Gardens of Babylon** Built in 605–562 B.C. by Nebuchadrezzar II, King of Babylon, it had multilevel gardens with machinery for circulating water. An earthquake destroyed it after the first century B.C.

- **Statue of Zeus at Olympia** A statue built in 435 B.C., it occupied the whole width of an aisle in a temple built in 466–456 B.C. It was destroyed in the fifth to sixth centuries A.D., presumedly by fire or earthquake.

- **Temple of Artemis at Ephesus** Built in 550 B.C., it was dedicated to the Greek goddess Artemis. Herostratus burned it down, but it was rebuilt, destroyed by the Goths, then rebuilt again. The final version was destroyed by an earthquake in 1303–1480.

Modern Wonders

Once you know the seven ancient wonders, let them inspire you to make up your own wonders of the modern world, based on your town, state, or places you have visited.

- **Mausoleum of Maussollos at Halicarnassus** A tomb built in 351 B.C. for Mausolus, a satrap in the Persian Empire. It was damaged in 1494 by an earthquake, and then disassembled by European crusaders.

- **Colossus of Rhodes** A huge 110-foot (34-m) tall statue of the Greek god Helios, built 292–280 B.C. and toppled by an earthquake in 226 B.C.

- **Lighthouse of Alexandria** At between 383 and 440 feet (117–134 m), it was one of the tallest man-made structures for centuries. Built in 280 B.C., it was destroyed by an earthquake in 1303–1480.

The Five Pillars of Islam

Why not use your time on hold to learn a little about another religion? In the Islamic faith, the five pillars represent the duties that are incumbent on any Muslim who wants to faithfully practice his or her religion. The pillars have an impact on Islamic societies, and sensitivity to these pillars is crucial for Western countries who seek involvement with them.

1. **Shahadah** Profession of faith.

2. **Salath** Ritual prayer, which must be practiced at five set times of day: dawn, noon, midafternoon, sunset, and night (about two hours after sundown). The penitent must face Mecca. In Islamic countries, the Call to Prayer is traditionally given by a muezzin, who climbs the minaret (tower) of a mosque and sings out "hasten to prayer," in a melodious call.

3. **Zakat** In this form of almsgiving, Muslims are obliged to give a fixed percentage of their income to the Islamic community as charity for the poor. This is a purifying act for the giver, as well as for the poor person who receives it, because the person on the receiving end won't need to beg.

4. **Sawm** Muslims must both fast and abstain from sex from dawn to sunset during the ninth month of the year, which is known as Ramadan.

5. **Hajj** Every able-bodied Muslim with sufficient funds (to cover both the journey and family expenses at home) is obliged to make a pilgrimage to Mecca at least once during his lifetime.

. . . .

"The strongest of all warriors are these two: Time and Patience."

—Leo Tolstoy
Russian writer (1828–1910)

The 10 Plagues of Egypt

The story of the 10 plagues is found in the Bible in Exodus 7:12. God sent ten plagues to the Egyptians when Pharoah, despite the pleas of Moses and his brother Aaron, refused to release the Israelites from slavery. Moses' mission to Pharoah is the subject of a spiritual, "Go Down Moses," and it is also used by William Faulkner (1897–1962) as the title of a short story collection about a family of slave owners. The last plague in this list is the one that finally brought Pharoah to his knees.

1. **Blood.** The Nile and all the water in Egypt are turned into blood, and all of the fish die, causing a terrible stench.

2. **Frogs.** Egypt is infested by frogs, which get into everything and corrupt the land.

3. **"Sciniphs"** (variously translated as gnats, lice, or fleas). Aaron strikes the dust with his staff and Egypt is overrun with flying insects.

4. **Flies.** These appear in a swarm.

5. **Pestilence.** This is an epidemic that kills horses, donkeys, cattle, sheep, and goats.

6. **Incurable boils.** Moses and Aaron scatter two handfuls of soot from a furnace into the sky and the Egyptians break out in purulent, incurable boils.

7. **A destructive storm.** Hail was mixed with fire.

8. **Locusts.** These consumed all the plants.

9. **Darkness.** It was so thick that it could be felt, lasting for three days.

10. **The death of the first born male in every family.** This plague affected everyone from humble servants to Pharoah himself.

READ YOUR **PALM**

Since fate has you in its grip while you wait for the capricious gods of customer service to answer your call, you can take the time to turn up your own palm to see what you can discern there. An occult fascination with palmistry has existed over the ages and is well documented in old paintings. You might not be able to supply all of the traditional atmospherics that accompany the image of a gypsy reading a palm. However, you can learn to trace the three principal lines on your palm and mull over some of the things they might tell you.

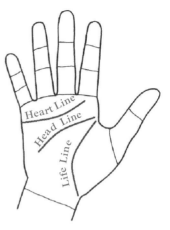

Heart Line
The upper line, starting near the index finger, represents your emotions and love life:

- A line beginning below the index finger indicates a tendency toward stability and contentment in love.

- If the line starts below the middle finger, you're more concerned with your own pleasure than your partner's.

- If it begins between the index and middle finger, it doesn't take much to make you fall for someone.

- A straight and short heart line indicates a forthright interest in sex, unclouded by sentiment.

- If it touches your life line, your heart is easily broken.

- A long, curvy line means you express loving feelings.

- If it is straight and parallel to the head line, you don't let your emotions lead you astray.

- A wavy heart line means a tendency to promiscuity.

- If a circle is on the line, your love life depresses you.

- Broken lines or smaller lines crossing through the heart line indicate emotional trauma.

Head Line

Found just below the heart line, this line represents your intellectual self:

- A short line means you express yourself best in athletic and physical, not intellectual, work.
- A curved, sloping line indicates an original thinker.
- If your head line is separated from your life line, you crave adventure.
- If you have a wavy line, your attention span is short.
- A deep, long head line indicates that you are an intent, focused thinker.
- If you have a straight head line, you don't let nonsense cloud your judgment; you're logical.
- A donut or cross in your head line means that you've experienced an emotional crisis that defines you.
- A broken line means you are impulsive.
- If there are multiple crosses through your head line, you've had to make many difficult decisions.

Life Line

The lowest line, this is the arc-shaped line that runs around the base of your thumb:

- A life line that runs close to your thumb indicates that you are often tired; your energy is low.
- If your line is curvy, you are a whirlwind of energy.
- A long, deep line indicates that you are a person with essential vitality.
- A short, shallow line indicates that your life is too influenced by other people.
- A life that swoops around in a semicircle means that you have a contagious enthusiasm.
- Multiple life lines is a sign of extra vitality.
- A circle in your line indicates that you have sustained an injury.

GIVE YOURSELF **A MANICURE**

If you aren't in a public situation where decorum is important (for example, at the front desk of a corporation), you can file your nails—if you have a speaker phone, that is! Hold your nail file at a 45-degree angle and file from the corner to the center of the nail in one direction, not from side to side. Stroke gently with an emery board. Don't saw at your nails as though you are cutting wood—and don't use a metal file, because they are unnecessarily harsh. The white part of your nail needs to be at least $1/8$ inch (2.5 mm) beyond the pink nail bed; filing very short nails will weaken them.

Still waiting on hold? Next take care of your cuticles. Start by soaking your fingertips in a bowl of warm, soapy water—add a couple of drops of dishwashing detergent, if you like. As you dry a finger, gently push the cuticle back with the towel, then use a cuticle pusher, a sticklike device with a soft tip—those made of wood, especially orangewood, are less damaging then metal ones.

. . . .

LEARN TO TAKE **YOUR PULSE**

Your pulse is the rate at which your heart beats, so it's an important number and one that you can easily take on your own. Athletes often take their pulse before and after exercise. Cardiovascular fitness is achieved when you exercise regularly to raise your heart rate to 50 to 75 percent of your maximum heart rate for a 20-minute period.

To take your pulse, you need a watch or clock with a second hand. The radial pulse is the easiest to locate: Take it on the inside of your wrist, in a straight line down from your thumb. Press your index and middle fingers over the pulse point (don't use your thumb, because it has its own pulse). Count the number of beats that you feel in 10 seconds, and multiply by 6 to get your beats per minute (bpm) rate. A normal pulse varies from 60 to 100 bpm, so you'll need to take it often (when you have five minutes) to get your personal normal rate.

Handy List for Hypochondriacs

Staring at your hands can lead to an important health check! Doctors know that hands can reveal clues to specific health conditions. Here are a few:

- Chronically hot or sweaty hands could be a sign of an overactive thyroid.

- Bony bumps around the finger joint near the fingertip are known as Heberden's nodes. These are bony or gelatinous bumps on the middle finger joints. Both are signs of osteoarthritis.

- Reddening of the skin on your palms, especially near your little finger, is known as palmar erythema and can signal liver disease.

- Shiny, tight skin on the hands and fingers is a sign of scleroderma, which is a connective tissue disorder.

- Clubbing, or an increase of soft tissue around the ends of the fingers, is linked to lung disease, liver cirrhosis, and inflammatory bowel disease.

- Splinter hemorrhages beneath the nails (thin, vertical red or brown lines) indicate bacterial endocarditis or infection of the heart valves.

- Dupuytren's contracture is a thickening of the tissues of the palm of the hand that causes the fingers to curve toward the palm; it usually affects the ring fingers and pinkies first.

- Fingers that blanch white or bluish, and then red due to sudden temperature changes might be a symptom of Raynaud's syndrome, a circulation disorder caused by blood vessels that overreact to temperature changes.

Note These symptoms do not mean you have a disease; always seek your doctor's advice.

SMILE SAFELY

Most dermatologists agree that habitual expressions, such as crinkling your eyes and forehead when you smile, can deepen furrows in the face. Therefore, some doctors suggest practicing smiling with just the mouth, while keeping the forehead and the rest of the face uninvolved. Botox performs a similar function by blocking the neurotransmitter that lets the muscles contract during such facial contortions as laughing, smiling, or frowning. You can be expressionless but unwrinkled—the choice is up to you! If you prefer fewer wrinkles, it's not easy to restrict a smile to a cautious upturn of the corners of the mouth, so you can practice while you're on hold.

. . . .

Feats for Fingers

If you spend any time thinking about your fingers, it's probably to schedule their latest manicure. Meanwhile, your fingers could be stiffening for lack of healthful exercise! Clever, flexible fingers are vital for tasks from the most mundane, such as tying a shoelace, to the most specialized, such as surgery or playing the piano or guitar. These exercises won't make your fingers as highly trained as those of a top-notch typist or a fine pianist, but they are a start:

- **Peacock's Tail Spread** Hold your hands joined in front of you, with all fingers tight together and thumbs hugging the index fingers as if you were praying. Like a peacock spreading its tail, stretch all five fingers as far apart as possible, and then furl them again. Repeat 10 times. This will improve your fingers' range of motion.

- **Resistance Training** Hold your hands in front of you, pressed together, fingers spread apart but touching from fingertips to palms. Using resistance between the fingertips, curve your fingers out in an arch while the tips continue to press against and resist one another. Repeat 10 times. Resistance training strengthens fingers and wrists.

- **Brain Calling Pinkie** Lay your hand down flat on a table or desk, with fingers spread easily apart. See if you can lift and arch just your middle finger and pinkie while the other fingers remain flat. Next try to lift and arch just your ring and index fingers. This surprisingly difficult exercise improves brain-finger communication and teaches your fingers to act independently of one another.

- **Rhythmic Finger Aerobics** Lay your hand flat on a surface, fingers spread apart. Imagine your fingers are numbered 1–4 (index through pinkie). Try to lift each finger separately in specific rhythmic patterns. The 4, 3, 2, 1 pattern is the easiest; then try 2, 4, 3, 1, and so on. Vary the patterns. When you have one set of fingers moving obediently to your brain's desires, see if you can bring in the other hand and move both sets of fingers simultaneously but in different patterns.

- **Newspaper Crunch** Crumple up newspaper with one hand, starting in one corner and continuing until it's all scrunched up. Try it. It's harder than it sounds. You can do it with one hand, and then the other.

- **Creating Vs** Violinists and other musicians practice these for finger position on strings. Start by holding your hands in front of you, with fingers together and straight. Make V's by stretching the fingers apart between the middle and ring fingers, keeping together the index and middle fingers, and also the ring fingers and pinkies.

  Now, keeping the index fingers and pinkies where they are, move together the middle and ring fingers, and then move them back to the previous positions. Do this a few times to limber up your fingers. If you're right handed, you might struggle to do this with the left hand, and vice versa, but keep trying—you'll be able to do it.

Naughty Fingers

See if you can unbutton your shirt—or someone else's—using the fingers from just one hand. This is, of course, best tried in private and with some discretion.

Waltz While You're Waiting

Instead of sitting hunched over the phone in frustration while you wait, cut loose with a few dance moves. If the on-hold music has a beat to it, that's all the better. Or why not try a basic box waltz, a ballroom dance with three beats to each measure, counted as "1, 2, 3"?

The steps for this basic waltz form a box shape, and the reach and slide movements of your feet will create a "dip and rise" effect. Keep your posture erect, with shoulders back. There are three steps of the same length in each measure. Waltz combinations are often described in a series of six steps, with the lead foot alternating, so simple instructions are given as "Right, 2, 3, Left, 2, 3." Once you master these steps, add a one-quarter turn to the left to each three-step combination. When dancing with a partner, he or she moves in the opposite direction.

Waltz Box Steps for Women

1. First set of three: Right foot steps backward (R1 on illustration). Count right.

2. Left foot steps back toward the right foot, but then glides to left (L2). Count 2.

3. Transfer your weight to your left foot and the right foot glides to meet your left foot (R3). Count 3.

4. New set: Left foot steps forward (L4). Count left.

5. Right foot slides forward toward the left foot, and then glides to right. (R5) Count 2.

6. Transfer your weight to your right foot, and the left foot glides right to meet it (L6). Count 3.

Note For men, start with the second set of 3 steps, then do the first set of 3.

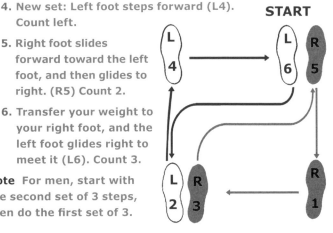

FIDGET AWAY **FLAB**

Of course you can easily work out while you're on hold—just pace! While you're at it, swing your arms or bounce your shoulders up and down, which will help to keep muscles in tone and burn up calories. Nervous types who pace or fidget can burn up to 500 extra calories a day, as well as raise their overall metabolic rate, when compared to their more placid counterparts. A study published in the journal *Science* determined that some people are naturally sedentary, while others burn about 350 more calories per day through "nervous" nonexercise activities.

. . . .

Exercise Quickies

You can choose from among these easy exercises below and on pages 34–35 to give your muscles a stretch. They will be easier to do if you have a speaker function on your telephone.

Toe Lifts
You can do these while either sitting or standing. You will need your shoes and socks off for this one.

1. **With your feet flat on the floor, start by lifting only your big toes off the floor while keeping the rest of your toes in contact with the floor.**

2. **Next try to keep your big toes on the floor and lift your remaining toes off the floor. Repeat 10 times.**

Mexican Toe Lifts
If you are able to master the basic toe lifts, you can progress to what is sometimes referred to as "the Mexican wave" for the feet. If you find this exercise difficult, you can start by using your hands to give your feet an idea of how it feels.

With your feet flat on the floor, try lifting each toe individually like a Mexican wave among a crowd at a ball game, placing each one down before lifting the next one. Try to create as much space in between each toe as possible.

Bicep Curls

If you have a water bottle (make sure the lid is secure), use it as a weight to perform this strengthening exercise.

1. Stand straight, with your shoulder blades down and back, your head centered over your neck, and your feet flat on the floor.

2. With your elbows tucked in at your side, start by flexing your elbow at a right angle while holding your water bottle in your hand, palm facing up.

3. Slowly straighen your arm and then bend it again. Perform three sets of 10 exercises on each side.

The Quadriceps

This exercise is for your quadriceps muscles—the ones along the front of your legs—to strengthen your knees.

   Sitting upright, be sure your back is supported and your feet are flat on the floor. Slowly straighten one leg and hold for the count of five. Next lower it slowly and with control. Repeat with the opposite leg; do three sets of 10 on each side.

Sitting Side Reaches

If you have a speakerphone, use it; otherwise, hold the phone in the opposite hand to the one reaching up.

1. Sit upright, with shoulder blades down and back and your weight evenly distributed through your backside.

2. Take a deep breathe in and lengthen through your spine. Keep facing forward—do not twist as you perform the movement. Lift your arm straight up above your head.

3. As you breathe out, reach up and across toward the opposite side, lifting up and out from the waist without compressing down into your opposite side. Keep both buttocks on the chair.

4. Breathe in and return to center. Rest and repeat in the opposite direction; do the same number of stretches on each side.

Sitting Twists

1. Sit upright, with shoulder blades down and back and your weight evenly distributed through your backside. Breathe in; as you do this you will feel your back lengthened.

2. As you breathe out, reach one hand across your body to the outside of your opposite knee or thigh. Slowly turn your head to mobilize your neck, looking over your shoulder as far as it feels comfortable. Keep your head in line with your spine as you do this—do not extend your neck.

3. Breathe in and out two to three times; return to the center. Repeat on the opposite side. Perform three to four times on each side.

Roll Downs

This exercise is good for stretching spinal joints. You can also do this exercise with your back against the wall and feet 12–16 inches (30–40 cm) away from the wall.

1. Stand with a good, centered posture, with your feet spaced hips' width apart and arms hanging straight down. Do not arch your back. Tighten your stomach muscles by drawing up your pelvic floor muscles.

2. Start with your head and neck by tucking in your chin and letting the weight of your head draw you forward. Roll down slowly one vertebra at a time, feeling the release of your tight muscles. Let your arms hang and breathe normally.

3. Roll down from your torso as far as it is comfortable. Support your hands on your legs, if necessary. Work at your own pace and don't overstretch.

4. As you return to the upright position, curl up slowly from the bottom of your spine. Think of "stacking your vertebrae one at a time" as you come up: lower back first, then middle back, shoulders, and finally your neck and head. Be sure you return to a good centered position before beginning again. You may find that you are able to roll a bit farther each time.

CHAPTER TWO

At Work

For some people, life at work is devoted to giving the impression—especially to the boss—that there is never five minutes to spare. In reality, the pace of the average 40-hour week veers unpredictably from breathlessly busy to interminably slow. Here are some suggestions for those suddenly empty minutes when the computer's down, the conference has been delayed, or you just can't face looking at another spreadsheet.

GET BEYOND A **POLITE SMILE**

Most of us know people that we see every day at work but barely acknowledge—perhaps with only a polite smile, a "have a good day," or "thanks a lot" as we buy our coffee, hand over our trash can for emptying, or grab our copies from the photocopying machine. If you have five free minutes as you storm through your day, now is the time to linger for some friendly conversation.

Simply asking someone how their day is going—and then taking the time to wait for and listen to an answer—might make a pleasant, warm minute in someone else's day and transform that acquaintance you see every day into a unique, individual friend.

....

Office Eagle Scout

Do a good deed for the day: Make a cup of fresh coffee or tea for a stressed-out office colleague and deliver it with a cookie or a piece of fresh fruit and a word or two of friendly encouragement.

....

"I would rather suffer with coffee than be senseless."

—Napoleon Bonaparte
French emperor (1769–1821)

....

PROFESSOR FOR A DAY

Take advantage of the special skills of your colleagues by organizing lunchtime forums—short courses taught by your coworkers in their areas of expertise. Lunchtime forums offer an opportunity for employees with particular experience, knowledge, or talent to pass on their know-how in a convenient time slot that doesn't overextend an already long workday. You can start planning a lunchtime forum course catalog in five minutes by sending around a sign-up sheet asking colleagues for input on forum topics they are capable of teaching.

Organize Your Time

Busy days at the office can be managed more efficiently if you organize yourself and your work. Take five minutes to note some of these suggestions:

- Get a spiral notebook from your supply room during a five-minute break. Keep it with you through the day and write down the things you need to do. At the end of the day, take five minutes to go through this book and organize a daily to-do list, putting the most important jobs at the beginning of the list.

- When planning your day, leave some free time to allow for interruptions and emergencies. Book 30 minutes with yourself, if necessary.

- If you're scheduling a meeting, be sure to also plan when it needs to finish. Try to insist on meetings ending when planned.

- At the end of the day, organize your work materials to be ready for the start of the next day, with the most important work placed on top of the pile. One article in the *Wall Street Journal* reported that executives wasted an average of an hour a day looking for mislaid papers.

- Delegate: If you can't do it all, make sure you arrange for important tasks to be handled by someone else.

. . . .

DE-LITTER YOUR **PURSE AND POCKETS**

Did you just run some work-related errands during your lunch break? In most offices it's important to keep receipts if you need to be reimbursed from the accounts payable department. Go through your purse or pockets, remove any old receipts and bill detritus, and double-check them, separating office receipts from personal ones. Shred those you don't need in a paper shredder. Organize the ones you need to save—make copies for your office's records, if necessary—and clip them together in a safe place to file at a later time.

Start an Acronym List

Do yourself and your coworkers a favor by starting an acronym definition list. You can pass it around the office and get input from everyone, and then publish it on the office website as a general reference. Keep in mind that depending on where the acronym is used, the same acronym can have different meanings. Here are some common ones to get you started. You can also use this eclectic list to play a new game—define that acronym!

AMA	American Medical Association
ASCII	American Standard Code for Information Interchange
ASTM	American Society for Testing and Materials
BPS	Bits Per Second
CDC	Center for Disease Control
CPU	Central Processing Unit
DOD	Department of Defense
DOT	Department of Transportation
EFT	Electronic Funds Transfer
EROM	Erasable Read Only Memory
FAQ	Frequently Asked Questions
FEMA	Federal Emergency Management Agency
GIGO	Garbage In Garbage Out
GUI	Graphical User Interface
HHD	Hand Held Device
HTML	Hypertext Markup Language
IAW	In Accordance With
IP	Internet Protocol
ISBN	International Standard Book Number
ISO	International Standards Organization
ISP	Internet Service Provider
KHz	Kilohertz
LANSAT	Land Satellite
MHz	Megahertz
NAFTA	North American Free Trade Agreement

NBS	National Bureau of Standards
NIH	National Institutes of Health
NTSB	National Transportation Safety Board
PIN	Personal Identification Number
PPM	Parts Per Million
UPC	Uniform Product Code
USDA	United States Department of Agriculture
WLAN	Wireless Local Area Network

Office Editor

Start a list of commonly misspelled or confused words. Post it on your bulletin board for office reference. You can update it in a future five minutes as necessary. Here are a few suggestions to give you a good start:

accommodate
a lot
all ready (fully prepared)
already (previously)
believe
born (to be given birth to)
borne (carried, endured)
calendar
changeable
collectible
complement (thing that completes or harmonizes with something else)
compliment (a nice remark)
definite
embarrass
harass
indispensable
its (possessive)
it's (it is)
judgment
liaison

millennium
mischievous
misspell
noticeable
occurrence
pastime
precede
principal (foremost in importance)
principle (rule)
rhythm
separate
stationary (immobile)
stationery (writing materials)
supersede
their (possessive)
they're (they are)
there (in or at that place)
twelfth
weird

Play with Typefaces

Do you always use the same boring typefaces for all of your office documents? Are you barely aware that there's a world of fonts beyond Arial and New Times Roman? Spend your five minutes experimenting with the smorgasbord of typefaces that your word processing program offers.

Common sense and caution are necessary—if you work in a sober law office, you don't want to produce your next memo in Edwardian Script or Goudy Stout. However, it can be fun to change the mood and style of your documents by using different typefaces. Just be aware that experimentation, until you become an expert, is best reserved for your personal documents—it's not a good idea on resumés.

"Never leave till tomorrow that which you can do today."

—Benjamin Franklin
American statesman (1706–90)

Make a Template

Use a software program to set up a format template for a letter, memo, or even e-mail—something that will save you time later when you are busy, but still want to send out a professional-looking document.

For the Commute

Print out an article that you want to read and tuck it into your workbag. That way you'll have it with you if you find time to read on the bus or train, or if you find yourself standing in line at some point.

Critique Your Company Website

Take a critical look at your company or department website and note areas of possible improvement.

. . . .

LEARN TO **TYPE À LA FRANÇAIS**

You can help your company with international communications—or your kids with their French or math homework—by spending five minutes learning how to type diacritical accents, mathematical symbols, Greek letters, and miscellaneous symbols, such as the © for copyright, in your word processing program.

Macintosh

Use the *Character Palette* supplied in Mac computers. To access it, open *System Preferences,* click on *International,* then click the *Input Menu* tab and add a check mark next to *Character Palette.* The *Character Palette* will open. You can choose the type of characters you need from the *View Pop-Up* menu at the top of the *Character Palette* window. You can also choose the font and type size that fits your document.

Windows OS

If you use a Windows operating system, the easiest way to type foreign language accents and special characters, such as square root (√), less than or equal to (≤), or Greek letters (useful in equations) is to click on *Insert* in your toolbar, then click on *Symbols and Equations.* A menu specific to the font you are using will pop up—all you need to do is click on your choice and hit *Insert.*

Another option is to open *All Programs,* then select and expand *Accessories,* select *System Tools,* and then *Character Map.* Again, an extensive and handy menu will open. You can choose the font and size to type your document in, select the character you want, and then copy and paste it into your document.

Beyond Control-Alt-Delete

Once you know computer keyboard shortcuts, they can save you a lot of time. You may need to experiment— what works in one program may not work in another program. You probably already use several favorite shortcuts all the time without thinking about it, but this list may contain some that are new to you:

Copying, Moving, and Deleting Shortcuts

CTRL + C Copy

CTRL + X Cut

CTRL + V Paste

CTRL + Z Undo

CTRL + A Select all

Shift Shortcuts

SHIFT + DELETE Deletes the selected item permanently without placing the item in the Trash

SHIFT when you insert a CD-ROM into the CD-ROM drive Prevents the CD-ROM from automatically playing

Arrow Shortcuts

RIGHT ARROW Opens the next menu to the right, or opens a submenu

LEFT ARROW Opens the next menu to the left, or closes a submenu

CTRL + RIGHT ARROW Moves the insertion point to the beginning of the next word

CTRL + LEFT ARROW Moves the insertion point to the beginning of the previous word

CTRL + DOWN ARROW Moves the insertion point to the beginning of the next paragraph

CTRL + UP ARROW Moves the insertion point to the beginning of the previous paragraph

CTRL + SHIFT + any of the arrow keys Highlights a block of text

SHIFT + any of the arrow keys Selects text in a document, or selects more than one item in a window or on the desktop

Control Shortcuts

CTRL while dragging an item Copies the selected item

CTRL + SHIFT while dragging an item Creates a shortcut to the selected item

F Shortcuts

F2 Renames the selected item

F3 Searches for a file or a folder

F4 Displays the *Address Bar* list in *My Computer* or Windows Explorer

ALT + F4 Closes or quits the active item

CTRL + F4 Closes the active document in programs that let you have several documents open simultaneously

F5 Updates the active window

F6 Cycles through the screen elements in a window or on the desktop

F10 Activates the *Menu* bar in the active program

SHIFT + F10 Displays the shortcut menu for the selected item

Alt Shortcuts

ALT + ENTER Displays properties of the selected object

ALT + TAB Switches between the open items

ALT + ESC Cycles through items in the same order that they had been opened

ALT + SPACEBAR Displays the *System* menu for the active window

Underlined Letter Shortcuts

Underlined letter in a command name on an open menu Performs the corresponding command

ALT + Underlined letter in a menu name Displays the menu

Escape Shortcuts

CTRL + ESC Displays the *Start* menu

CTRL + SHIFT + ESC Opens *Task Manager*

At Work

Upgrade Your Skills

Use the *Help* menu in computer programs to teach yourself new tricks.

Unforgettable Passwords

Be sure to regularly change your accounts' passwords or PIN numbers to enhance security. To help yourself remember the new passwords, make up mnemonics. For example, if you have two children, a password can be made from a combination of letters and numbers designating the dates of their births, such as: 828605112613. This may seem like a random number sequence to someone else, but to you it means your two children were born in the years 1982 and 1986, in May and November, on the 26th and 13th days.

The origin of the word mnemonics is Mnemosyne, the Greek goddess of memory. Mnemonics have been used for centuries to jog the memories of forgetful humans: "Every Good Boy Deserves Fudge" has been the time-honored staple of music teachers teaching the order of notes on the lines of the treble clef. And if you have trouble spelling mnemonic, what better way to remember it than this sentence: "Monkey Nut Eating Means Old Nutshells In Carpet." In fact, you can create a memorable mnemonic sequence for just about anything that is crucial to remember.

TIME FOR AN **UPDATE**

If you work for a small business or at home, you might need to be a computer expert. Many software manufacturers offer free updates, made to get rid of glitches in earlier releases. Don't confuse these with "upgrades," advanced versions of the software that require a payment. The best time to download free updates from the Internet is before a break, because they can take a while to download. If your computer has a password, be sure to enter it before you take your break, or you'll return to find the computer asking for a password!

Clean Your Keyboard

Once you've hovered over an office computer keyboard for a few months, it becomes a visible reproach for all your snacking sins and a veritable museum of the detritus of office life—dust, hair, crumbs, splashes of coffee, and the buildup that is generally described as gunk or grime. If your keyboard is looking icky, here is a safe way to clean it in five minutes. Keep the supplies as office necessities in your desk drawer; however, if you don't have them, ask that analyst across the aisle with the spotless cubicle:

- cotton swabs
- 70 percent isopropyl alcohol
- a can of compressed air
- disinfecting wipes

Steps to a Clean Keyboard

1. Disconnect the keyboard.

2. Turn it upside down and shake it over your trash can. Watch the gentle rain of crumbs, dust particles, grit, and if you're lucky, those paper clips that somehow found their way to the keyboard's deepest interior.

3. While still holding the keyboard over the trash can, use the compressed air according to the manufacturer's directions on the can, and enjoy the sight of dislodged clots of dust flying from the niches of your keyboard.

4. With the keyboard once again upright on your desk, dampen the cotton swabs with the isopropyl alcohol and swab between the keys to clean away the gunk.

5. Use the disinfecting wipes to gently wash the grime from the top surface of the keys.

Keep the Keys Clean

One alarming British study suggested that computer keyboards are more germ infested than bathroom toilet seats.

REFRIGERATOR CLEAN-OUT DAY

Is your office refrigerator full of malingerers—food items that have been languishing on the crowded shelves for weeks? It's time to put the owners on notice that the end of their aging snacks is approaching. E-mail your colleagues a polite but firm notice stating that all food that is not labeled with a name and date will be thrown out on the upcoming Friday, so that the refrigerator can be cleaned. At the same time, talk with your colleagues and have them agree that henceforth, Fridays will be refrigerator clean-out days—when all unclaimed food will be tossed in the trash.

. . . .

Destatic Your Computer Monitor

The same destatic ingredients in dryer sheets that work for your clothes will lift away hair and dust from your computer monitor. Keep a spare box in the office for periodic cleanups.

. . . .

Dust Thou Art. . .

Offices are dusty places and the main reason for that is they harbor lots of people! The major component of interior dust is dead human skin cells. The average human sloughs 30–40 skin cells every second. Add shed hair; fibers released from carpets, fabric cubicle partitions, and clothing; the dust mites attracted to the dead skin cells; and dust mite fecal matter, and you've got dust bunnies scampering around computer cords.

The best defense is to use a vacuum cleaner with a High Efficiency Particulate Air (HEPA) filter, and make sure that you also vacuum the partition walls of your cubicle if they are made of fabric. If you use a cloth to dust, use a treated dust cloth or clean cotton cloth lightly dampened, and dust from the top to the bottom so that the dust you dislodge does not fall onto a clean surface. And don't forget to dust around your computer.

Clean Up Your Universe

Once a hectic project comes to an end, you might take a look at your work area and be horrified at the sight of what has accumulated in the chaos. Here are some tips to clean up your desk:

- Weed out the papers on your desk. Shred those that are no longer needed, file those you'll want later, and settle the rest in strategically arranged stacks or vertical desk storage bins.

- Put away pens, paper clips, and other supplies.

- Organize the files on your computer before turning it off for the day.

. . . .

PRIME **YOUR SUPPLIES**

Get into the habit of checking the office supplies at your desk the first Monday of every month. Load your stapler with staples, and make sure you have a fresh roll of tape if the one on your tape dispenser is about to run out. Next empty your three-hole paper puncher of all the little punched out paper circles. Test your pens and pencils, discarding the ones that no longer work. There's nothing more frustrating than having to stop during a rushed job to do one of these tasks.

. . . .

Endless Envelopes

Make interoffice envelopes reusable even when all the spaces have been filled in. Simply tape a sheet of paper on the front and back of the envelope, and label the sheets with "To" and "From" columns. This trick allows interoffice envelopes to be used indefinitely—or until they split at the seams.

Q: How did the cubicle start?

A: The father of the modern office cubicle is Robert Propst, a Michigan designer who launched the Action Office in 1968 as a system of desks and cabinets, the first design for creating multiple modular offices in one large room. Propst's office was designed with varied height surfaces—so that workers could work standing up when they were tired of sitting—and shelves. However, economy-minded companies stole the idea of movable partitions and shrunk them to cram in as many workers as possible, giving birth to modern cubicle culture.

. . . .

Release Your Cubicle's Life Force

Feng Shui—the literal translation from Chinese is "wind-water"—is a set of aesthetic principles said to use the natural forces of heaven and Earth to unblock the flow of chi, or life energy. Even if you have only five minutes and just a little control over your office environment, you can unleash some feng shui arrangements that will free up the chi that's clogged in your cube!

- **If possible, sit with your desk facing the entrance. This powerful position enhances the flow of confident chi. If you must sit with your back to the entrance, use a mirror that reflects what is happening behind you.**

- **Arrange any seating in your office space in a triangle facing your desk, emphasizing that your desk is the center of power.**

- **Increase the sense of warm light (a beneficent natural force) by using a lamp with a natural glow, a small mirror, or a crystal paperweight.**

- **Create a mood of calmness and peace with water—a tiny electric fountain would be nice, but in a pinch, even a photograph of flowing water helps.**

- **Provide gentle natural sounds by using wind chimes, a small bell, or a bamboo flute.**

- **Plants near the door will draw good chi into the area.**

> "Coolness and absence of heat and haste indicate fine qualities."
>
> —Ralph Waldo Emerson
> American poet (1803–82)

At Work

QUICKIE MENTAL **MATH TRICKS**

Some people seem to work out the answers to mathematical problems faster than you can reach for a calculator. Perhaps they are using one of these shortcuts, which you, too, can learn in just a few minutes:

The quick way to multiply by 9

Think of it as multiplying by (10−1). So, to multiply 68 × 9, for example: 68 × (10−1) = 680−68 = 612.

Multiplying by 5 or 25

Multiplying by 5 is like multiplying by 10 and dividing by 2. To multiply by 10, simply add 0 to the end of the number you are multiplying by. So for example, 5 × 85 = 850 ÷ 2 = 425.

To multiply by 25, multiply the number by 100 (add two zeros to the end of the number), then divide by 4. So for example, 25 × 46 = 4,600 ÷ 4 = 1,150.

How to square a two-digit number ending in 5

The square of any two-digit number ending in 5 will always end in 25. To calculate the rest of the sum, take the left digit (say, 7 in 75, for example) and multiply it by one more than itself. So to calculate the square root of 75: 7 × 8 = 56; then add 25 as the last two digits. The square root of 75 is 5,625.

How to square a three-digit number ending in 5

For a three-digit number ending in 5, take the two left digits and multiply them by one more than the number they represent. So to calculate the square root of 765, for example: 76 × 77= 5,852. Add 25 to the end of 5,852. The square root of 765 is 585,225.

 51

Already Metric?

Aspirin, wine, and soft-drink bottles are already sold in metric units. Mechanics need metric tools to repair imported vehicles and appliances.

Everywhere in the world except for Myanmar, Liberia, and—that other geographic outpost—the United States, uses the metric system as its primary system of measurement. You can prepare for the eventual triumph of the metric system in the United States by learning some conversions in your spare few minutes. Here are the formulas:

Celsius to Fahrenheit Multiply the Celsius temperature by 9, divide it by 5, then add 32, or (degrees C × 9 ÷ 5) + 32 = degrees F.

Fahrenheit to Celsius Deduct 32 from the Fahrenheit temperature, multiply it by 5, then divide by 9, or (degrees F − 32) × 5 ÷ 9 = degrees C.

Length

To change	Into	Multiply by
inches	millimeters	25.4
inches	centimeters	2.54
feet	meters	0.305
yards	meters	0.914
miles	kilometers	1.609
millimeters	inches	0.039
centimeters	inches	0.394
meters	feet	3.28
meters	yards	1.09
kilometers	miles	0.621

Area

To change	Into	Multiply by
square inches	square centimeters	6.45
square feet	square meters	0.093
square centimeters	square inches	0.155
square meters	square feet	10.8

Dry volume

To change	Into	Multiply by
cubic inches	cubic centimeters	16.4
cubic feet	cubic meters	0.0283
cubic yards	cubic meters	0.765
cubic centimeters	cubic inches	0.061
cubic meters	cubic feet	35.3
cubic meters	cubic yards	1.31

Liquid volume

To change	Into	Multiply by
fluid ounces	milliliters	29.5735
cups	milliliters	236.588
pints	liters	0.473
quarts	liters	0.946
milliliters	fluid ounces	0.0338
milliliters	cups	0.0042
liters	pints	2.11
liters	quarts	1.06

Weight

To change	Into	Multiply by
ounces	grams	28.4
pounds	kilograms	0.454
tons	metric ton	0.907
grams	ounces	0.035
kilograms	pounds	2.2
metric ton	ton	1.1

At Work

. . . .

"Like as the waves make towards the pebbled shore, So do our minutes hasten to their end." —William Shakespeare
English playwright (1564–1616)

Give your brain an occasional challenge to keep it active. Stash a tough crossword or Sudoku puzzle in your desk drawer, and work on it for five minutes whenever you feel the need for a mental change of scene.

Bushwhack Your Brain

Your brain is crossed by a network of worn paths, but it has uncharted territory, too. By going where you don't usually go, you can create new mental trails in your brain, blazing fresh connections for electrochemical communication between nerve cells.

If you're at work, walk through a maze of cubicles in an unaccustomed pattern, or use your opposite hand to control the computer mouse, to engage your mind and enable electrochemical impulses to slip from synapse to synapse. Brain researchers refer to this desirable ability of the brain to quickly cross-categorize as neuroplasticity. Here are some other simple tips to try:

- **In the cafeteria, identify the coins to pay for your coffee by feel instead of sight—as long as there isn't a long line of coworkers behind you.**

- **Eat your lunch with your opposite hand. You'll have to eat slowly, which is better for digestion.**

- **Practice mirror or looking-glass writing: Try to write a few sentences backward, so that they would appear correctly if held up to a mirror. (Lewis Carroll and Leonardo da Vinci both practiced mirror writing.) This is not advised for technical reports.**

- **When you get in the car to go home, see if you can fasten your seat belt and find your key—and put it in the ignition—all with your eyes closed.**

The Mind Is Its Own Place

A mind map is like your own personal flowchart, but without the fussiness. While business flowcharts strictly map processes, a mind map charts the thoughts, impulses, and emotions that swirl around a particular issue in your mind. The purpose of a mind map is to get these skittering fragments written down on paper where you can look at them as a whole and see where things are heading using colors, shapes, whimsical connectors, even decorative borders and marginal illustrations.

Start with a central issue that's been on your mind—for example, is it time to ask about a promotion or do you need to wait? Write that issue in the center of your paper, inside whatever type of shape you fancy, and inscribe the burning question in whatever manner you prefer.

Next, as if you were brainstorming a school paper, add the issues, emotions, ideas, thoughts, and feelings that surround the force field of the central topic in your mind. If you have colored markers or other art materials available, use them. You can connect and branch off topics however you feel will be appropriate. You and only you will know when your mind map is complete. Keep your map inside your desk drawer, and refer to it as an aid to analyzing your problem.

LEXICOGRAPHY LITE

Page through the office dictionary and get to know some of its fine points. Most common hardcover dictionaries have lists of historical names, geographical places, and a history of the English language. It's illuminating to read the etymologies, or histories, of words, which often reach back many years.

START A **FREE OFFICE LIBRARY**

If your office has a break room or lunchroom where there's space for a bookcase, bring in books and magazines that you no longer want and start an office exchange. Your colleagues will catch on and bring in their own offerings. It's best to take a free-for-all approach to the reading material: If you want it, it's yours, but bring in replacements. Exchanging publications is a great way to save everyone a little money, declutter your house, and widen your reading horizons.

....

"They talk of dignity of work. Bosh. The dignity is in leisure"

—Herman Melville
American author (1819–91)

....

How Do You Say Stapler in French?

Label all your office surroundings with sticky notes that give their name in a foreign language. Here are a few examples in French:

book le livre
business card la carte de visite
chair la chaise
clock la pendule
computer l'ordinateur
desk le bureau
eraser la gomme
felt-tip pen le feutre
file (computer) le fichier
file (paper) le dossier
highlighter le surligneur
letter la lettre
memo le mémoire

paper le papier
pen le stylo
pencil le crayon
stapler l'agrafeuse
tape le ruban
telephone le téléphone
wall le mur
window la fenêtre
window blind le store

BEYOND **FAMILY SNAPSHOTS**

If you spend long hours each week at your cubicle desk with little to look at besides a computer screen and a bulletin board, why not put some of that bulletin-board real estate to work improving your mind? Make yourself some cards inscribed in bold letters with anything you'd like to memorize: a poem, French verb conjugations, Sir Isaac Newton's three laws of motion, words to a song you want to learn—the choices are vast. You can use part of your five minutes to download some material from the Internet.

Post the cards on your bulletin board somewhere near your family photos, where you'll catch glimpses of them throughout the day. Soon you will be able to recite the content in your sleep. When you feel that you've reached the limit of what the cards can teach you, make up a new set with some new items to absorb.

At Work

. . . .

Filing Shortcuts

During chaotic periods it's not unusual for folders to be filed away erroneously, perhaps a B being mistaken for a D in the file cabinet. When you have a few minutes to spare, work your way through the files, a letter of the alphabet at a time, to put the files in the right order. If there are particular files you use all the time, highlight the tabs with a bright color to make them easier to find.

. . . .

MAKE A **RUBBER-BAND BALL**

Rubber-band balls can grow to an impressive size—enough to play a rousing round of office basketball. To start the ball, you need a core: a small piece of paper crumpled into a hard-ball shape. Start wrapping the rubber bands around the core, being careful to avoid whiplash from snapping bands. Wrap them from different vantage points, so that your ball stays in a spherical shape.

Redesign Your Desktop

Pick out a new background for your computer desktop, choose a new screen saver, and change the icons.

Last-Minute Sewing Kit

Keep some thread and needles in your desk drawer to fix a popped button—and safety pins to hold closed a broken zipper.

Mend Your Jacket Button

A button has popped off your jacket— and you have a presentation later in the day. You know how to sew on an ordinary button, but if the jacket material is thick, you may need to create a shank with the thread to keep the material from puckering when buttoned up. Here's how:

1. Make a pair of stitches through the button and fabric as you would with a normal button, but keep them loose.

2. Holding the button about ¼ inch (5 mm) away from the fabric, make about six stitches per button hole.

3. Wrap the thread several times around the stitches between the button and fabric—this forms the shank—then secure the thread in the fabric and knot as you would for a normal button.

....

Answer at Large

When planning a presentation, include a few minutes of preparation time to think about questions that may be asked by the audience. Here are a few pointers to help you out when answering questions:

- Make sure that the entire audience has heard the question (you'll probably have to repeat it). Direct your answer to the entire audience—not solely at the person asking the question.

- Avoid the trap of being so grateful for any questions that you let one person monopolize you in a one-on-one dialogue, without letting everyone have a chance to participate.

Know Your Speech in a Flash

To prepare for a speech or presentation, take some index cards, or fold pieces of paper into a convenient size, and make yourself a set of flash cards. Copy important phrases from your speech or presentation to help you memorize them. Refer to the cards whenever you have a few minutes to spare, and you'll soon have your speech imprinted on your brain.

. . . .

GET IN A **PRACTICE SESSION**

If you have a few minutes to spare before a PowerPoint presentation, ask a friend to skim your electronic slides, choose two at random, and read you the headings on the slides. Then talk to your friend about what is on the slides—you won't be able to read or parrot them, and you'll have to speak about the points to a person, instead of staring at and talking down to the slides—a major presentation faux pas.

. . . .

ENGAGE AN **ACCOMPLICE**

If you are new to public speaking and feel that you need all the help you can get, there's nothing wrong with organizing some sideline coaching. Take five minutes and ask a friend who will be attending the presentation to tip you off with some prearranged cues if you are taking too long, mumbling, shouting, or reverting to nervous tics, such as fidgeting with the change in your pockets.

. . . .

Prowl the Premises

If you're near your presentation venue, take a sneak peek at the room. You need only five minutes to note where you will stand and the distance from the audience, so you'll have an idea of the volume at which you need to speak. Note if there's a lectern available, and think about where you might place any props, such as a laser pointer.

At Work

Swivel Chair Olympian

You can hone a challenging skill simply by thinking about it—all in the comfort of your own cubicle. While sitting quietly in your chair at the office, imagine yourself perfectly performing a difficult feat, such as a tricky tennis serve or a speech before a large audience. Studies support the idea that mental rehearsal, or practice, is a valuable supplement to the real thing.

To begin, sit quietly and visualize yourself performing the skill. Let your body experience what it feels like—for example, if the skill is horseback riding, remember the way the horse moves your seat through the saddle and let your sensory memory participate and respond. For your presentation, imagine yourself speaking confidently in front of a group of people, standing with good posture. Imagine yourself dealing with any surprises—a spook of the horse or an unexpected question—with consummate skill.

Researchers have discovered that muscles get stronger when you imagine exercising them. They theorize that the muscles improve because the brain becomes more adept at "talking" to them through mental practice!

Q: What is the world's largest office building?

A: Don't think that the world's tallest building is also the largest office building. The world's largest office building, the Pentagon—the headquarters of the U.S. Department of Defense—has over 3.7 million square feet (343,750 sq m) of space and a 5-acre (2-ha) central plaza. Some 23,000 employees work in the building, located in Arlington, Virginia.

Feet Flat, Back Straight...

Many jobs today demand working on a computer for long hours, which can strain your muscles, particularly your back, neck, and shoulders. To avoid injury, make sure your computer and office furniture are positioned correctly and that you sit at them with the right posture. Even if you're busy, take five minutes to do this check:

- Be sure to sit with your chair close to your desk—stretching places strain on your shoulders.

- Adjust your seat height so that your lower arms form right angles with your upper arms at the elbows and that your arms are relaxed at the sides of your body.

- Make sure your forearms are slightly above the desk and parallel to it.

- Check your hands—they need to form a continuous line with the forearms, not bent up or down.

- Position your hips so they are slightly higher than your knees, but keep your feet flat on the floor.

- Make sure that your back is supported by your chair—if not, use a rolled-up towel or a small cushion behind your lower back.

- Check the angle of your backrest—it needs to incline slightly backward, not forward.

- Your eyes must be level with the top of your display screen, which needs to be directly in front of you.

- Position your keyboard 4 inches (10 cm) from the edge of the desk—again, directly in front of you.

- Place your mouse within reach to avoid stretching.

. . . .

SCALE THE STAIRWELL

To fend off the late afternoon can't-stop-yawning spell, take a five-minute walk outside, or if you're in a big office building, go to the stairwell and scale as many flights of stairs as you can conquer in five minutes.

Nadi Shodhana

Many office buildings are notorious for poor air quality—the result of many people crowded into spaces with no natural flow of air. If you find yourself becoming drowsy, headachy, or congested, try a five-minute break outdoors.

While enjoying the fresh air, you can practice the alternate nostril-breathing technique known in Sanskrit as *nadi shodhana,* or "channel cleaning." An aspect of yoga breathing techniques, *nadi shodhana* is said to enliven the mind by clearing the breathing channels and increasing oxygen flow to the brain. Here is the simple exercise:

1. Curl the index and middle fingers in toward your palm on your dominant hand. Then place it so that your thumb rests by one nostril and your ring finger and pinkie are by the opposite nostril.

2. Close off alternate nostrils by pressing with the near finger (thumb or ring finger) while taking a steady slow, full breath in through the opposing nostril.

3. Close off the nostril you just breathed in and exhale slowly, steadily, and fully through the opposite nostril. Breaths and exhalations should last about 8 seconds each. Be sure to alternate nostrils. Do 6 to 10 cycles.

. . . .

"Take rest; a field that has rested gives a bountiful crop."

—Ovid
Roman poet (43 B.C.–A.D. 17)

HANDY **MASSAGE**

If you type, write, or use tools, your hands are exposed to frequent stress. A hand massage will release tension not only in your hand but also in the arm, shoulder, and neck that are connected to your hand by nerves. Applying a hand lotion or essential oil first will make your skin more supple and add a nice scent.

Start at the base of the fleshy pad below your thumb. Use the thumb of your opposite hand to rub small, firm circles, and work your way up to the tip of your thumb. Next use the opposite thumb to make firm, gliding strokes from the bottom of each finger, applying pressure in the gaps between the four metacarpal bones, going toward the wrist. Finally, use your opposite thumb and index finger to pinch—applying firm but never painful pressure—the tips and then the sides of your fingers, working up and down the fingers.

. . . .

A Nudge in the Right Direction

Do you feel a tension headache coming on? Discover the soothing power in your own hands by trying the ancient Chinese healing art of acupressure. To apply acupressure, use your finger, thumb, or knuckle to apply a massage or pressure to acupressure points on your body. Acupressure is believed to stimulate the meridian system, or the network of nerves that branch throughout your body, to release and rebalance the nerves' natural energy forces, known to the Chinese as yin, yang, and chi. Here are just a few of the acupressure points on your body:

- **For claustrophobia** On the groove of your inner wrist, in line with your thumb.

- **For a tension or anxiety headache** The point on your middle finger, just below your nail, on the side closer to your thumb.

- **For a sinus headache** On the cheek, just beside the curve of your nostril.

Note Remember that acupressure is intended as a supplement to health care—it is not a replacement.

Five-Minute Desk Workout

For the sake of your back and neck, take a five-minute break every hour to do some stretches. Perform these exercises slowly and carefully; stop if you feel any pain.

1. **Stand and stretch** Put the heels of your hands on your lower back and pull your elbows back. Keeping your head in line with your spine, slowly arch your back until you see the ceiling.

2. **Shoulder stretch** Link your fingers and press your palms away from you, so your shoulders and upper back are rounded. You will feel a gentle stretch in your forearms, fingers, and the muscles between shoulder blades. Hold for five seconds; repeat.

3. **Finger and wrist stretch** Hold your arms straight in front of you, facing each other. Make a soft fist with one hand, and then gently place your other hand over it and give a slow and gentle stretch. Hold for four counts. Repeat with the other hand.

4. **Diagonal stretch** Sit slightly forward in your chair with your right hand reaching slowly toward the left side of your chair at elbow height. Hold for four counts. Repeat to the opposite side.

5. **Shoulder circles** You can do these sitting or standing. Pull your shoulders up toward the ears, then let your shoulders drop down and back, squeezing the shoulder blades together. Relax. Next pull your shoulders toward each other in front, up toward the ears, then relax. Repeat four times each way.

6. **Head and neck stretch** While sitting in an upright position, imagine a thread from the top of your head gently pulling you up. Slowly tuck your chin in, making a double chin and feeling a gentle stretch along the back of your neck; hold for the count of four. Repeat four times.

7. **Neck rotations** Assuming the upright posture as in stretch 6, slowly turn your chin toward your right shoulder, then to the left four times.

A Mental Break

Many people work long hours but—let's be honest—they would often rather be somewhere else. The feeling of being trapped in one place can build up until stress responses reach a dangerous level. When that "tied to my office chair" feeling gets too strong, don't let your stress overwhelm you. Instead use the power of your own mind to take a (nondrug-induced) trip—letting your brain generate visual, auditory, tactile, and scent sensations to create a strong mental experience of a place where you'd like to be—limited only by your imagination.

Sit quietly and comfortably, and focus on deep, regular, controlled breathing and the progressive tensing and then releasing of muscles in an orderly progress from your head down to the toes.

Meanwhile, let all of your senses work in imaginative concert to take you to a different place. Perhaps it is a pine forest, where you see the towering evergreens with their reddish trunks rising to a rich Christmas-green hue, with a wonderful balsam scent as your bare feet revel in the soft, deep cushion of pine needles that muffle all but the gentlest sounds of the trees swaying in the wind. It takes time to become skilled at this type of relaxation, but with patience and diligence you can learn the pleasures of mental journeys to help reduce your stress levels.

At Home

When you have five unscheduled minutes, you may
not know what to do first. No matter how small
or how spacious it is, any home will offer a dizzying
panorama of tasks vying for your attention. This
chapter offers suggestions, from the utterly industrious
to the pleasingly frivolous. Some will help you focus
so you know where to turn; others will provide you
with inspiration to try something new. Whatever
you choose, expect it to be satisfying.

YOU'RE **RICHER** THAN YOU THINK

The average home has at least $5.50 in loose change hiding—in pockets, behind couch cushions, forgotten in old purses, and of course, at the bottom of the washing machine. Your five minutes of loose time might be a good opportunity to corral your change and put it in a bag or jar to cash in at the nearest coin-counting machine. In fact, $5.50 is probably a conservative estimate of the idle riches squirreled in the hidden recesses of your home. A 16-ounce (450 g) glass jar of coins holds about $28.54—more than enough to pay for a pizza or even a nice bottle of wine.

. . . .

Clean House

Juggling home life with a career? Bringing order to chaos at home doesn't have to mean a week's worth of serious cleaning crammed into a few hours over the weekend. Just five minutes' worth of well-chosen tasks sprinkled through the week can help you take control of your home. Here are some suggestions:

- **Dust the tops of baseboards and other moldings in a room—don't forget the door.**

- **Clean door handles and light-switch plates with disinfecting wipes.**

- **Shake out a throw rug.**

- **Dust the slats in a window blind with a dryer sheet. Its ingredients will lift away hair and dust motes—those particles that can be seen floating around in the air.**

. . . .

CORD SAFETY

Do a one-room electrical cord safety check. Inspect the cords to make sure they are not frayed or cracked, do not run under rugs, are securely plugged into their outlets, and do not feel hot to the touch. Then check that the outlets are not overloaded (no more than two appliances to an outlet). If there is an extension cord, make sure it is the correct gauge for the appliance connected to it and it is not plugged into an overloaded adapter.

A Sparkling Window

Of course, cleaning all of the windows in your home will take more than five minutes, but you can tackle one window at a time to break up the task into five-minute blocks. Try some of these suggestions to make window cleaning easier:

- Choose a cloudy day to wash a window—streaks on the window will show up better than on a sunny day.

- If curtains are in the way, hang clothes hangers on the curtain rail, then hang the curtains in the hangers. (You can do this in preparation for cleaning the window later in the day.)

- You can make your own window-cleaning solution by adding 2 tablespoons of vinegar to warm water in a spray bottle.

- Use crumpled newspaper to dry the window. Not only is the paper absorbent, but the ink will also polish the glass.

- Use horizontal strokes for polishing one side of the window and vertical ones for the other, so you'll know which side of the window has any streaks.

Candle in the Wind

Test a window for drafts by holding a lit candle near its frame. If the flame flickers, the window may need weatherstripping or caulking.

At Home

....

"Do something every day that you don't want to do; this is the golden rule for acquiring the habit of doing your duty without pain."

—Mark Twain
American writer (1835–1910)

Try Being Orderly

There are several areas around the house that easily become cluttered. When you have five minutes to spare, tackle one of these at a time to declutter, and eventually you'll have a clutter-free home. Here are some suggestions, but you're bound to think up your own:

- Rifle through your coat and jacket pockets looking for things you've forgotten.

- Try to make sense of the household junk drawer: throw away, re-home, or sort the drawer's contents.

- Go through your jewelry box to pair up your earrings.

- Organize your mail pile and trash any junk mail.

Wallet Time
Go through your wallet to remove any receipts and expired coupons that have built up since its last clear out.

END **MANUAL MADNESS**

Gather together all of your appliance manuals for the next time you need instructions— whether it be a simple maintenance job or a breakdown that calls for a pro. Get rid of manuals for appliances you no longer own, and make a list of missing manuals. Write down the model, make, and number, then the next time you have five minutes, download and print out the manual from the Internet. Don't forget to add the manual to your collection.

PUT YOUR **KEY CHAIN** ON A DIET

Do you lug mystery keys around on your key chain? (What could they be for—perhaps your 1985 college dorm room?) Does your key chain drag down the waist of your pants when you stick it in your pocket? If the answer is yes, then it's time to retire some of the chain gang. Remove all the keys that you don't use or recognize. If you harbor a fear that someday you'll find a keyhole that needs a key, store the extra keys in a drawer. Excessively heavy key rings can actually damage the starter on your car, so lighten the load before you need to visit a car mechanic.

WEED OUT **YOUR CLOTHING**

Go through a closet or drawer and purge it of things that you never wear and don't really like. You'll be surprised how streamlined and efficient you will feel afterward. Either put the things in the trash or in a bag for charity. If you choose a charity, carry the bag to the car so that you really will drop it off. If you have children, you'll be familiar with the regular need to weed out clothing they have outgrown. Store these for a younger sibling or donate them to a thrift shop or charity.

. . . .

Now for the Books...

Organize your bookshelves by author or subject, an ongoing project that you can work on whenever you have five minutes. At the same time, weed out some books. Remove those that you found boring, and discard or put them in a box for the library or a charity. Again, take them immediately to the car for drop-off.

. . . .

...and CDs

Sort through your music CDs, classify them, and make sure they are all in the correct plastic jewel boxes—also an ongoing project. The next time you want to listen to U2, you won't be annoyed when you open the jewel box, only to find your son's Jay-Z CD!

. . . .

BASKET PATROL

Expecting guests at short notice? Use your laundry basket to quickly gather up any clutter around the house, and hide it in a closet. Once your visitors leave, put things away in their rightful places.

Make Things Whole Again

Get out some glue to mend a mug, figurine, or other object that's been broken for months. If this fails, it's really time you consider discarding it!

The Indispensable Vacuum Cleaner

If you normally rush through rooms vacuuming only your carpets, take this opportunity to concentrate on the often-missed areas. Tackling one room at a time, vacuum in the corners where dust and animal hair tend to collect. Use the vacuum crevice attachment to clean under couches, beds, bookcases, and cabinets. Run a long-handled vacuum cleaner attachment (or a broom) around the ceiling to remove dust, cobwebs, insects, and spiders.

When you have another spare five minutes, remove your couch and chair cushions to vacuum under them. You might try reaching down in the crack between the back and seat as well—there's no telling what you'll find! Changing your vacuum cleaner's dust bag is something else you can do in five minutes or less.

CHEAP **CLEANERS**

Mix up your own inexpensive, nontoxic household cleaner. Vinegar is an effective natural cleaner and deodorizer, and because it is acidic, it will cut through grease. Add about 2 tablespoons of vinegar to 1 quart (1 liter) of hot water, and wipe away greasy spots in the kitchen with a rag wrung out in the solution.

Make a Polish

Try making your own furniture polish to nourish your (nonantique) wood furniture with a rubdown, without using chemicals. Mix ½ cup (125 ml) of olive oil with ¼ cup (60 ml) of lemon juice. You will need to apply the solution on the same day that you make it, using a soft cloth.

BRIGHT **LIGHTBULB** IDEA

If you haven't gotten around to changing a burned-out lightbulb, now is the time. And what better time to look into an energy-efficient compact fluorescent lightbulb (CFL) that qualifies for an energy star from the government. They use about 75 percent less energy than a normal incandescent bulb—and last 10 times longer! They come in different sizes and shapes, so spend five minutes choosing the appropriate type for the room and its use. CFLs work best in open fixtures, such as pendants and lamps. There are special types available for a recessed fixture, as well as for a lighting fixture with a dimmer or three-way switch.

....

De-Fur Your Refrigerator

You and your trusted vacuum cleaner can help keep your refrigerator's need for electricity under control. The condenser coils, found either on the back or the bottom of the unit, are how the refrigerator dissipates the heat it removes from the interior of the refrigerator.

Kitchens, as crossroads of activity and the favorite lounging place of family pets, tend to send a lot of dirt, dust, and hair under the refrigerator, coating the coils and reducing their ability to dissipate heat. The refrigerator motor has to work much harder to do its job. To remedy this, unplug the refrigerator (for safety), then use your vacuum's crevice attachment to clean the coils, removing as much coil-insulating hair, dust, and fur as possible. You'll be a lot happier the next time you tear open the monthly electric bill.

....

Q: Which is one of the most energy-hungry appliances?

A: In the home, the refrigerator is responsible, on average, for about 20 percent of a domestic utility bill.

Spick-and-Span Refrigerator

Use one of these suggestions to clean your refrigerator.

- Go through the shelves and bins to weed out expired items.

- Spot clean the interior of the refrigerator with baking soda, warm water, and a sponge or rag.

- Rinse the bottles (such as jelly, mustard, and ketchup) in hot water to remove any sticky residue.

Dishwasher Day

Time-Saver

Using a dishwasher instead of washing dishes by hand can save you three weeks of time in a year—and it's more hygienic because the water temperature is higher.

Just before you turn it on, open your dishwasher and gaze at the crowded racks. Imagine washing each of those messy dishes, and feel gratitude for your appliance. Here are a few hints to help keep your dishwasher slaving away for you:

- Use a soft brush to clean the gaskets around the door and frame. Food debris can cause a poor seal, causing water to leak out.

- Inspect the interior to be sure that the water sprayer, screens, and filters are not clogged by food or mineral deposits.

- Give the dishwasher a bath by putting 1 cup (225 ml) of vinegar in a dishwasher-safe cup on the lower rack and running the empty machine through a wash cycle.

CLEAN YOUR **GARBAGE DISPOSAL**

Boil a kettle of water to have it ready. Add ½ cup (125 ml) of baking soda to the disposal, then 1 cup (225 ml) of distilled white vinegar. Let this mixture sit for a few minutes, then pour the boiling water down the disposal. Or pour down 2 tablespoons of chlorine bleach, then flush with cold water.

Perk Up the Coffee

Sluice your electric coffeemaker of the stale sludge that sours the coffee. Fill the glass carafe halfway with distilled white vinegar, then add water to the top of the carafe. Run the solution through the brew cycle, then repeat with clear water.

LEMON FRESH

If you have a stained wooden cutting board, the next time you have five minutes free, try squeezing some lemon juice over it. You'll need to let it stand for a few hours or overnight; however, you'll find that the board will be much easier to clean when you return to it.

RENEW A **SMELLY SPONGE**

You can microwave your kitchen sponge to disinfect it. Put the wet sponge in the microwave and turn it on—1–2 minutes set on high is adequate, but keep an eye on the sponge just in case it burns. When the microwave heats the water, it will kill the bacteria, which makes the sponge smelly. Let the sponge cool before removing it.

Hone a Knife

1. Start with the heel (wide end) of the blade at the base of a steel sharpener. Your hands will be near each other; your dominant hand holding the knife and the other hand holding the steel.

2. Draw your hands apart, pulling the blade across the steel sharpener at a 20-degree angle. Using an even pressure, draw the entire cutting edge of the blade across the steel, ending with the blade's point at the tip of the sharpener.

3. Make strokes on both sides of the steel, so each side of the knife is sharpened. Hone to the desired sharpness, usually 6–10 strokes across the steel.

At Home

Honey-Mustard Vinaigrette

Here's a classic salad dressing that is simple to make in just five minutes.

1. Pour $^1/_4$ cup (60 ml) of cider vinegar into a large, screw-top jar. Add ¼ teaspoon of salt and a good grinding of black peppercorns, along with 1 teaspoon of Dijon mustard.

2. Put on the lid securely and shake well to blend. Add 2 teaspoons of honey. Cover and shake again. Taste for sweetness and add more honey if you like.

3. Pour in 1 cup (225 ml) of extra-virgin olive oil a little at a time, shaking well after each addition to make it emulsify. Refrigerate and use as desired.

Low-Fat Creamy Dressing

Although this salad dressing will stay fresh in the refrigerator for only a day or two, it's worth the minimal effort it takes to make this quick-and-delicious dressing. Serve it over a crisp salad.

1. Pour ½ cup (125 ml) nonfat yogurt into a bowl.

2. Finely chop 1 scallion, then add to the bowl along with 1 teaspoon of dried oregano, 2 teaspoons of Dijon mustard, and salt and pepper to taste. Stir well. Cover and refrigerate until you're ready to use it.

Homemade Russian Dressing

You won't want to buy a store-bought dressing loaded with preservatives after making this delicious recipe at home.

1. In a small bowl, mix 1 cup (225 ml) of mayonnaise, ¼ cup (60 ml) of ketchup, and 1 teaspoon each of horseradish and Worcestershire sauce, along with ½ teaspoon of salt and ¼ teaspoon of ground white pepper.

2. Stir the mixture until thoroughly blended, then spoon into a large airtight jar. Refrigerate and use as needed.

Garlic Butter

Make this seasoned butter ahead of time, then cut off slices to make garlic bread or flavor vegetables.

1. Cream 8 tablespoons (1 stick/225 g) of softened butter with a wooden spoon in a small bowl.

2. Peel 2 cloves of garlic, then chop finely. Pour over ½ teaspoon of salt, and use the side of the knife blade to work into the garlic until crushed to a paste.

3. Scrape the crushed garlic into the creamed butter; stir to mix thoroughly.

4. Place it on some plastic wrap and roll into a sausage shape roughly 6 inches (15 cm) long. Refrigerate the butter until needed.

....

Chinese Pepper Rub

This easy rub is particularly good on spareribs.

1. Place 1 cup (55 g) of black peppercorns and ¼ cup (15 g) of green or red peppercorns in a sealable sandwich bag. Crush with a rolling pin, then pour into a large screw-top jar.

2. Add 1 tablespoon of red pepper flakes, ½ teaspoon of Chinese five spice powder, 2 tablespoons of brown sugar, and 1 tablespoon of salt. Screw on the lid, shake, and store in a cool, dry place until needed.

....

At Home

5 Fast Snacks

- Hummus with carrot and celery sticks
- Cherry tomatoes stuffed with tabbouleh
- Apple stuffed with cream cheese and raisins
- Berries, grapes, and melon chunks topped with vanilla yogurt mixed with a little honey
- Peanut butter and banana sandwich

Oaty Crumble Topping

Surprise your family with a crisp fruit crumble for dessert. If you have five minutes during the day, you can make the crumble topping ahead of time. It's delicious, and it will make your house smell fantastic while it's baking in the oven!

1. Pour 1 cup (85 g) of rolled oats into your food processor. Process for about 30 seconds, until it looks like coarse sand.

2. Add 4 tablespoons (½ stick/50 g) of butter, ½ cup (100 g) of brown sugar, and 1 tablespoon of cinnamon. Process until well blended. Put the crumble mixture into a bowl, cover, and refrigerate.

3. When you are ready to finish the dish, fill a shallow 9-inch (23-cm) square pan halfway with sliced apples or pears. Cover with the crumble mixture, and bake in a preheated oven at 350°F (180°C) for 30 minutes, until the fruit is soft and bubbling and the crumble topping is crisp and golden.

Berry Blast

Put ½ cup (75 g) of blueberries, 1 teaspoon of sugar, and 1 cup (225 ml) of plain yogurt into a blender and blend. Pour into a glass and enjoy.

Make Designer Ice Cubes

Add a maraschino cherry, a chunk of pineapple, or a sprig of fresh mint to the squares of an ice cube tray, fill with water, and freeze. These will make nice ice cubes for a cool drink.

> "The discovery of a new dish does more for human happiness than the discovery of a new star."
>
> —Anthelm Brillat-Savarin
> French gourmet (1755–1826)

Sweet-and-Sour Chicken

Get a head start on dinner by putting meat into a sealable plastic bag with a marinade for up to 24 hours. This one will develop a delicious sweet-and-sour flavor.

1. Put either 4 chicken pieces, 4 chicken breasts, or 8 wings or drumsticks into a sealable bag.

2. Add ¼ cup (60 ml) each of soy sauce, sesame oil, and pineapple juice, and ¼ cup (50 g) brown sugar, plus pepper and ¼ teaspoon of Chinese five spice powder. Seal the bag, shake, and mix so that the chicken is thoroughly coated. Refrigerate.

3. To cook, pour the chicken into an ovenproof dish and bake in a preheated oven at 350°F (180°C) for 40 minutes. The juices should run clear when the chicken is pierced in the thickest part with a skewer.

....

Five-Minute Meatloaf

Quick cleanup and no chopping makes this a dinner you can get ready in a dash. You won't need a mixing bowl—but you'll have to get your hands dirty.

1. Put 1 pound (450 g) of ground beef into a loaf pan. Crack in 1 egg, add 1 teaspoon of salt, ½ teaspoon of ground pepper, 4 ounces (115 g) of store-bought salsa, and ¼ cup (35 g) of store-bought bread crumbs. Squish together with your hands, being careful not to let the mixture fall out of the loaf pan. If you are a messy worker, do this in a slightly larger, oval-shape dish. It will make a flatter meatloaf, but you will have a cleaner counter.

2. Smooth the top to make a dome shape. Wash your hands, then run a moist paper towel around the edge of the pan. Cover with plastic wrap, and refrigerate until 40 minutes before you are ready to eat.

3. Bake in a preheated oven at 350°F (180°C) for 30–40 minutes.

At Home

Reduce Medicine Cabinet Clutter

An overstuffed medicine chest is a dangerous invitation to taking the wrong medication, or one that has expired. You can clean out your cabinet in five minutes by simply checking labels and expiration dates. However, grab some duct tape, and most important of all—stay away from the toilet! Medicines flushed down the toilet are one reason our waterways are being polluted by a toxic stew of drugs, including antidepressants, hormones, and antibiotics.

If your county or municipality has a Toxic Waste Disposal Day that accepts drugs, then secure all unwanted medications in a safe, sealed container until you can bring them to the disposal program. Otherwise, wrap duct tape around all containers securely, put them in a sealable bag, and dispose of the bag in the trash—preferably in the garage, not the kitchen. This method isn't perfect, but it will help to protect streams and groundwater, because modern landfills have liners and caps to reduce the amount of toxins that leach into the soil.

Emergency!

Post the poison control center phone number in a prominent place in your bathroom or kitchen, so it's easy to find in a hurry.

BATHROOM LIBRARIAN

If you keep magazines or books in a display rack in the bathroom, take five minutes to update the collection and retire some of the more outdated, well-used reading materials.

Clean the Grout

Mix some baking soda with water to make a paste, and use an old toothbrush with the paste to scrub a small area of grout between a few tiles. By doing a small area at a time, it becomes a less daunting task.

SPARKLING CLEAN **MIRROR**

Abrasive chemicals can damage your bathroom mirror. For a pristine mirror, make your own nonabrasive solution: Mix ¼ cup (60 ml) of distilled white vinegar with 1 cup (225 ml) of warm water—this can be strong smelling, so make sure the room is well ventilated. Or mix together ½ cup (125 ml) of rubbing alcohol, ⅔ cup (150 ml) of water, and 1 tablespoon of ammonia. Apply either solution with a sheet of crumpled-up newspaper, and rub in circular movements across the mirror. Use a dry sheet of crumpled-up newspaper to remove any drips before they dry.

Makeup Is Not Immortal

Wish that you had an excuse to indulge in some new cosmetics? Consider these facts: Most experts agree that makeup has a limited shelf life. For health reasons, discard makeup that is past its prime—especially eye makeup, and in particular mascara, which can cause eye infections as it ages and becomes contaminated with bacteria. You can weed out the aging beauties from your cosmetics bag or drawer in five minutes. Here are the suggested life spans of common cosmetic products:

Mascara 3 months
Eye shadow 1 year
Eye and lip pencil 1 year, if sharpened frequently
Lipstick/lip gloss 1 year
Liquid or cream foundation 3 to 6 months
Blush 6 months
Powder 1 year
Facial cleansers/moisturizers 6 months

At Home

SHAMPOO YOUR **HAIRBRUSH**

To clean your hairbrush, first use a wide-tooth comb to remove any trapped hair. Next soak the brush for a few minutes in a sink filled with warm water and a capful of ammonia or a few drops of shampoo. Drain the sink, rinse the brush thoroughly, and set it upright to dry.

Slow Drain

If water is draining away slowly, grease or hair may have accumulated in the drainpipe. Try using a bent length of wire to remove the blockage. If the wire doesn't work, pour ¼ cup (55 g) of baking soda and ½ cup (125 ml) of vinegar into the drain, let it fizz, then pour in 4 cups (1 liter) of boiling water. If this also fails, try the plunger before calling the plumber.

SANITIZE YOUR TOOTHBRUSH HOLDER

Give your toothbrush holder, whether it is a ceramic rack, tumbler, or plastic tube, a good wash in hot, soapy water or a weak bleach solution. While you're at it, consider whether your toothbrush is past its expiration date. Toothbrushes need to be replaced every three months for maximum teeth-cleaning utility and sanitation.

Laundry Duty

Try these suggestions to speed up doing the laundry:

- Collect dirty laundry and take it to the washing machine for when you can do a load.

- Separate the items into piles by color and fabric—put dry-cleaning items to one side.

- Put delicate scarves or panty hose in a pillowcase to keep them from being tangled up.

Clean Your Iron

To clean a sticky plate on the bottom of your iron, use a small dab of toothpaste on a soft cloth. Rub stubborn marks gently with steel wool. For an iron with a nonstick plate, using a soft cloth, clean it with detergent and water or methylated spirits.

Practice a Challenging Laundry Fold

The tricks of the trade for neatly folded laundry is something that your mother may have taught you. However, if your mother was otherwise engaged, here is a small tutorial on one of the more befuddling laundry folds—how to fold a fitted sheet:

1. Hold the sheet up so that the short-side corners of the rectangle are in either hand.

2. Next pocket the left top and left bottom and right top and right bottom corners inside each other.

3. Once the corners are neatly pocketed, lay the sheet on a large flat surface, such as a bed or table, smooth the sheet, and fold the ends with the pocketed corners over so that the pockets disappear into the fold and the sheet's edges are squared.

4. Smooth the sections of the sheet that conceal the pockets, then fold as you would a flat sheet.

....

> "The laundry has its hands on my dirty shirts, sheets, towels, and tablecloths, and who knows what tales they tell."
>
> —Joseph Smith
> American religious leader (1805–44)

....

VALET SERVICE

Check your wardrobe to see what can use a little spiffing up. In five minutes, you can defuzz a sweater with a battery-powered pill remover or a disposable razor. Or brush a suit or dress with a clothes brush or a lint roller. Other options are to polish a pair of shoes or iron a pair of pants. You can also sew on a button that has come off a jacket, shirt, or skirt. Once again, you'll be able to wear that blazer that you've been avoiding because it's missing a button.

At Home

Cleaning Gems

If you have just five minutes, you might have time to clean your jewelry. However, first make sure that your treasured pieces don't contain gems that can be ruined by the cleaning process. Here's a guide to what can—and cannot—be cleaned at home:

Diamonds, rubies, and sapphires Add a few drops of ammonia and two drops of dishwashing liquid to a bowl of hot water. Put your ring into a tea strainer and dip it into this mixture briefly, then rinse in cold water.

Jade Wash in soapy water and dry with a soft cloth.

Emeralds, opal, and turquoise These soft stones absorb water and may crack. Have them cleaned professionally.

A Sterling Luster

You can reduce the amount of tarnish sterling silver jewelry develops by storing it properly. Silver tarnishes when it is exposed to certain elements in the air. When you are not wearing it, store it on its own in a sealable plastic bag. When you have five minutes to spare, rub it with a soft cotton or flannel cloth to clean it. Or use a silver cleaning cloth impregnated with antitarnish ingredients.

Light Dirt

If your sterling silver jewelry has some light dirt or makeup that needs removing, mix a little liquid detergent in ½ cup (125 ml) of warm water. Use a soft cotton or flannel cloth to apply the mixture to the jewelry. Rinse it off with clean, warm water before drying it completely. If there are any tiny details, use a soft child's toothbrush to gently clean inside them.

UNTANGLING A KNOT

If you have a fine chain that is knotted up, here's how to untangle it. Place it on a sheet of wax paper, and add one or two drops of baby oil. Use two sewing needles to gently tease out the knot.

FOR HUMANS, **NOT FOR PETS**

There are foods that are safe for you, but not your faithful dog or inquisitive cat. Spend a few minutes memorizing these items to make sure your pet is kept safe. For your trusting canine, keep anything with chocolate, coffee, garlic, onions (and onion powder), macadamia nuts, bread dough, avocado, and grapes and raisins out of reach. For your finicky feline, chocolate and onion should not be in its diet, but also keep acetaminophen, antifreeze, rotting garbage, wood tar derivatives, tea tree oil, turpentine or mineral spirits, rodent baits, and weed killers out of reach—of course, these last items are not for human consumption either!

. . . .

Feline Soccer Practice

Make a toy for your cat by concealing some catnip inside an old sock and tying a knot in the end. Cats love batting these "soccer balls" around.

. . . .

REFRESH YOUR PET AND HIS DOMAIN

Take the dog or cat outside and give him or her a good brushing. Do it outside (or in the basement or garage) so you won't have to clean up the hair afterward. Shake out the dog's bed and sweep underneath—it tends to get a bit dirty under there. Give the area a spray with a safe, natural flea-control product.

. . . .

Petting a Pet

Spend a few minutes stroking or massaging your dog or cat. Many studies have shown that stroking a pet lowers your blood pressure. Massaging a pet is also beneficial to the pet's health, as well as your mutual relationship.

Organize the Garage Interior

Is your garage so packed with stuff that it makes you think of a jungle? Is your car unable to penetrate the dark interior? Start your garage deforestation project by dividing the garage into zones—sports, garden, automotive, recycling, and so on—and whenever you have a spare five minutes move some items into the correct zone. While you're moving the items, think about your storage options—shelving, hooks, containers— and note what you'll need to buy to store the items efficiently. Here are a few suggestions to get you started:

- Buy plastic trays to go under spillable things, such as paint cans.
- Get a lockable cabinet for toxic substances.
- Hang a Peg-Board for storing hand tools.
- Fill a pail with sand and vegetable oil to store garden tools—oily sand keeps the tools sharp and rust free.

. . . .

Prepare Your Lawn Mower for Winter

- Drain the gas from the tank.
- Use a wire brush to remove caked-on grass.
- Add a small amount of clean oil to the spark plug hole.
- Apply spray oil to the other moving parts to help prevent corrosion during storage.

. . . .

Q: How many people keep a car in their two-car garage?

A: According to the U.S. Department of Energy, of homes with two-car garages, 25 percent of the people don't park cars in their garages and 32 percent have room for only one car. Another survey says 50 percent of homeowners rate the garage as the most disorganized place in the house.

CHECK YOUR **ENGINE OIL**

Before checking your engine's oil, make sure the car is parked on a level surface and the engine has been turned off for at least two minutes to let the oil settle. Pull the dipstick all the way out from the holder. The dipstick will have a hollow, round handle, like a keyhole. Wipe the dipstick with a paper towel or rag, then stick it back where it came from—all the way. Pull it out again and read the oil level—the oil will adhere to the dipstick.

What Color?

Clean oil is a golden brown, somewhat clear color. Dark, dirty-looking oil means you need to drain and replace it soon.

Oil at the "full" mark (farthest line from the pointed end) is good. Oil ending at the lower line (nearest line to the pointed end) means you need oil. Even if it's a bit down from the full line, add a little oil of the manufacturer's recommended grade, then recheck. Be careful not to overfill.

INSPECT YOUR **TIRE TREADS**

Tire treads worn down to about a $1/16$-inch (1.5-mm) depth are unsafe, illegal, and must be replaced. To check the condition of your tire treads, you can use an ordinary penny. Insert the penny into the groove of the tire tread. If Lincoln's noble visage is at least partly smothered by the tire tread, your tread is legal. However, if all of Lincoln's mournful gaze is out there uncovered by tire tread, he's telling you something, in oracular tones—it's time for new tires.

Tires also have wear bars—raised bands of rubber inside the tread. If a wear bar is exposed, it is time for a new tire.

At Home

> "Law of the Workshop: Any tool, when dropped, will roll to the least accessible corner."
>
> —Author Unknown

Step Back in Time

Pull out an old photograph album that you rarely get a chance to look at, and spend a nostalgic few minutes revisiting good times and beloved persons of the past. Or, if you haven't added your latest photos, you can use these few minutes to do so.

A Big Day

Pique your children's intellectual curiosity by making a list of events that happened on their birthdays. If you have access to the Internet, compile the list by going to www.brainyhistory.com, or do a search using the phrase "history for kids."

LET ME TELL YOU **A STORY**

Give your young children a sense of their roots by telling them a quick story about an aspect of the lives of their grandparents or great grandparents. Helping children understand that life did not start with them develops their sense of compassion for others and stimulates their interest in history.

FIVE POINTS FOR **MOM'S MAIDEN NAME**

Have your children create a family trivia game. Supply them with a package of index cards and some colored markers and encourage them to come up with family-related trivia questions, perhaps assigning graduated points for easiest to hardest. While this will take you only five minutes to get them started, it will keep your children occupied for a lot longer.

It Was a ____ and ____ Night

Engage your children in some yarn spinning by writing a fill-in-the blank story. Dash off a few pages of an adventure, but leave spaces to be filled in by your kids. Ask them to write some nouns, adjectives, and adverbs on slips of paper, fold them up, and put them in a bowl. They can pull the words out randomly to fill in the blanks.

MAKE A **MÖBIUS STRIP**

Named for August Ferdinand Möbius, a German mathematician, the Möbius strip is a one-sided, flowing surface that has only one edge. It is easy to make and will amaze younger children:

Cut a strip from the 17-inch (43-cm) side of an 11 × 17-inch (28 × 43-cm) sheet of paper. On one side, label the four ends:

A	C
B	D

Give the rectangular strip a half twist and join the ends A to D and B to C. Tape them together. You have a Möbius strip.

To show a child that the strip has only one side, use a pen to draw a line along the strip, not lifting up the pen. The entire strip will be marked when you return to your starting point, although you did not lift your pen. If you cut the strip in half lengthwise, instead of becoming two pieces, it will become a single loop with two half twists.

Fan Belts

Car fan belts were once fashioned like Möbius strips, because the single flowing surface was more durable than a two-sided belt.

· ·

Root Some Veggies

The next time you are chopping fresh carrots with their leafy tops, ask your children if they would like to start a windowsill carrot garden.

Cut off the carrot (use one that is a good size) around 1 inch (2.5 cm) below the crown—the end with the leafy top. Leave 1 inch (2.5 cm) of the leaf stem attached to the crown but remove the outer leaves. Plant in a medium-size (5-inch/12.5-cm) clay pot, covering all but the very top of the crown and stem in potting mix. Set it in a partly sunny kitchen windowsill and keep it moist. In about a month, your child will be rewarded by the sight of the carrot's new, attractively lacy foliage. This technique will also work for other root vegetables, such as parsnips and turnips.

Design a Rebus Game

A rebus is a puzzle that uses graphics, usually combined with words, parts of words, or letters, to represent another word or phrase. Rebuses were popular on Victorian greeting cards and were also used on the television game show *Concentration*—the contestants had to guess a word or phrase from parts of words and graphics that were slowly revealed on a board.

Your rebus can be designed so that the relative position and size of the letters, parts of words, or words and graphics—as well as their arrangement in relation to one another—will also provide clues to the rebus. For example, a picture of a large man, imposed on a picture of an old-fashioned campground, with a plus sign and the word "us," might represent "Big Man on Campus."

If you lack illustration talent, which might make your drawings difficult to decipher, cut out pictures from magazines, newspapers, and old greeting cards to make a rebus. Create a rebus each time you have five minutes to spare, until you have enough of them to sit down and play a guessing game with family and friends. This is a fun project to get your kids involved in, with each family member making cards.

BOTTOMS UP TO **BETTER DRAWING**

One way to draw better is to observe your subject objectively. To challenge your powers of observation, draw a common object that you've turned upside down. Upending your customary perspective enables you to see the object that is in front of you without putting a label on it and, thus, unconsciously trying to draw your preconceived idea of it. The best subjects to draw in this way have plenty of detail, so that your eye will be challenged. See how much detail you can capture in just five minutes.

Arrange a Still Life

You can create a traditional arrangement of flowers, leaves, and grasses in a rustic pitcher. Use a sharp knife or scissors to cut the stems at an angle, and strip off any leaves that would sit below water level—the water needs to be tepid. Consider the size of the flowers to their container, and choose a few dramatic flowers for a focal point. Or settle some beautiful fruit in a wooden bowl, with an eye to their colors, shapes, and textures.

. . . .

Dry Flowers for an Arrangement

Keep forgetting to water the plants? Replace them with a dried flower arrangement—created by you. On a clear, dry day, pick a few bright flowers and leaves. Choose small flowers that form in clusters, such as baby's breath and yarrow. Remove all but one leaf near the blossom, then secure a small bundle with a rubber band. Find a dark, dry, and well-ventilated place to hang them for two to four weeks. Presto—they will be dry but not brittle!

. . . .

> "He enjoys true leisure who has time to improve his soul's estate."
> —Henry David Thoreau
> American writer (1817–62)

. . . .

PRESSED FLOWER GREETINGS

For a personal touch, press flowers to decorate your own greeting cards. For fleshy flowers, lay each blossom between two pieces of absorbent paper; if the blossoms are delicate, use wax paper. Place in a warm, dry place, and use books or bricks to weigh down the flowers for four weeks. As another five-minute filler, use a toothpick to dab some white glue on the flowers and press them onto a card.

Involve the Kids in Menu Planning

Ask your children for some ideas for the next week's family dinner menus. If the kids make the wrong suggestions, discuss healthy eating with them. If you haven't thought much about U.S. Department of Agriculture (USDA) food guidelines, then you have some review work to do. Since the inception of U.S. government-sponsored food advice in 1894, there has been a steady de-emphasis on the importance of meat protein and dairy products; clarification that the "grain group" refers to whole, not refined, grains; and controversies over fat and alcohol recommendations. Some highlights over the years include:

- **1943** The "Basic Seven" food groups introduced, with the "Recommended Daily Allowances (RDAs)."

- **1956** Food groups reduced to the "Basic Four": milk, meat, fruits and vegetables, and grain products.

- **1977** In "Dietary Goals for the U.S.," the Senate Select Committee on Nutrition and Human Needs begins to de-emphasize fats, cholesterols, sugars, and sodium—food types linked to chronic disease.

- **1995** First official recognition that a vegetarian diet can meet all RDAs.

- **2005** The USDA pyramid allots stripes to the five food groups; the wider the stripe, the higher the amount of daily calories to be chosen from that group.

For interactive activities related to the food pyramid for both you and your children, visit www.mypyramid.gov.

....

Q: What is linked to fewer behavioral problems in kids?

A: Regular family meals at home are the best predictor of fewer behavioral problems and better test scores—even more so than time at school, studying, or sports.

Reducing Morning Mayhem

Getting the family out the door for the day ahead can be like running a marathon. Here are some tips, each of which you can do in just five minutes, for making the mornings a little bit easier:

- **When you put away laundry, store your child's school clothes in "complete outfit" stacks. Your child will be able to quickly choose an acceptable outfit on busy school mornings.**

- **Set up your coffeepot the night before, so that all you have to do in the morning is plug it in or turn on the burner. If you have a programmable coffeemaker, set it to brew in the morning.**

- **Spend a few minutes at the end of the day making sure your child's backpack is loaded with all the necessary gear (permission slips, notebooks, school books, pens and pencils, bus pass, mittens) that will be needed for the next day.**

....

FOR THE **SINGLE HOUSEHOLD**

Even singletons may need extra time in the morning to arrive at work more relaxed, perhaps even with enough time to stop for a coffee on the way. Do a five-minute prep the night before. Decide what to wear and make sure that your chosen outfit has no wardrobe malfunctions (stains, hem down, missing buttons, broken zipper, run in tights) and that you have the right (won't show) underwear and accessories.

....

...And Minimizing Dinnertime Chaos

If you have five minutes before you leave for work, set the table for that night's dinner. Or prepare some dinner ingredients ahead of time. Set dried beans to soak for a homemade soup or casserole. Or peel potatoes and place them in a pan filled with cold water—you can do this the night before if stored in the refrigerator.

At Home

Prepare For a Night by the Fire

Set the stage for a lovely evening in front of a crackling fireplace blaze. You can lay the fire in a few minutes' time before you leave home on a winter's day and have it ready to ignite when you return home cold and tired. Here's how:

1. The fireplace floor should be bedded in ashes or sand to a 1–2 inch (2.5–5 cm) depth.

2. Lay a large log—the "back log"—horizontally along the back of the fireplace (preferably on a grate).

3. Place kindling—crumpled newspapers, resinous fatwood, or wood shavings—in front of the back log.

4. Place another log similar to the back log in front of the kindling—this is the "front log."

5. As though you were crossing an "H," lay another log across the back and front logs. When you return home, start the fire by lighting the kindling—be sure that the fireplace flue is open before you strike the match!

···

"My bounty is as boundless as the sea,
My love as deep; the more I give to thee,
The more I have, for both are infinite."

—William Shakespeare
English playwright (1564–1616)

Dash Off a Love Letter

Not a romantic poet like John Keats (1795–1821)? You can use his work as a model to write your own five-minute love letter. Keats wrote in a rush but made his point in a mere two paragraphs.

> To Fanny Brawne:
> I cannot exist without you—I am forgetful of every thing but seeing you again—my Life seems to stop there—I see no further. You have absorb'd me.
>
> I have a sensation at the present moment as though I were dissolving . . . I have been astonished that Men could die Martyrs for religion—I have shudder'd at it—I shudder no more—I could be martyr'd for my Religion—Love is my religion—I could die for that—I could die for you. My Creed is Love and You are its only tenet—you have ravish'd me away by a Power I cannot resist.

....

The Five-Minute Solution
Romantic Countdown

If you come home from work in a loving frame of mind, you can set some speedy romantic hints that even the most prosaic partner will be sure to notice. Although it would be practically impossible to do everything on this list, you'll be able to do two or three of these suggestions to set the right mood:

- Grab the mail before your partner gets home and put it aside.

- Pick some flowers from the yard—anything small and natural will do. They are more charming than florist flowers.

- Set a mood with lighting. Dim the overhead lights, and light a candle or two.

- If you drink wine, get two glasses ready.

- Choose some music to establish the right mood. Try to select something that is unobtrusive but soothing.

At Home

SIMPLY **SYBARITIC**

How decadent can one be in five minutes? Given the time constraints, it's probably safe to go the limit and see just how luxe you can be. Grab a bonbon or two, lounge in your squooshiest chair, and read something entirely frivolous and fascinating—perhaps a tabloid awash in photos of Brangelina. Your career as a voluptuary will be up in five minutes, so make the most of it.

. . . .

Simmer Your Feet In Salts

Let's say you've just come home from a long day at work, with high-speed errands on the way home, and now you're due out the door again in five minutes to a PTA or town meeting. You don't even have time for a shower, but you feel in need of pampering. Try a foot soak.

The age old Epsom salts (magnesium sulfate) soak has been proven to increase blood magnesium levels. Magnesium is absorbed through the skin during soaking, and the mineral is said to help the body maintain levels of serotonin, a mood-elevating chemical. No wonder foot soaks are so soothing! To increase the pleasure, add essential oils, such as rosemary, pine, lavender, or peppermint.

A simple soak recipe Add 1 cup (225 g) of Epsom salts to a small tub of warm water with a drop or two of the essential oil of your choice. If you want to make a practice of foot soaking, gather small smooth stones and add them to the bottom of the soaking pan. They'll provide a massage as you soak. Enjoy for five minutes!

. . . .

"He does not seem to me to be a free man who does not sometimes do nothing." —Cicero

Roman statesman and author (106–43 B.C.)

Calling the Relaxation Response!

The body's relaxation response is the opposite of its fight or flight response. Think of fight or flight as how you feel when you get ready for a stressful meeting by dressing to the nines with full makeup, and relaxation as when you wear your oldest, most comfortable nightgown. The relaxation response lowers your blood sugar, blood pressure, breathing, and heart rates. Here are some easy five-minute methods to court the relaxation response:

Brush your hair Even a simple, repetitive stimulus like gently brushing your hair with a natural bristle brush will help. Brush gently so that the brush doesn't rip at the hair, but firmly enough to massage the scalp.

Scalp massage Give yourself a simple scalp massage by pressing gently but firmly with the pads of your fingers and making small, regular circles. Start at your forehead, then move to the temples, and down to the nape of your neck. Alternate the circles with sweeping strokes using all five fingertips stretched from the temples to the forehead and arching over the top of your head and back to the nape of your neck.

Meditate Here's a simple meditation for a quick break. After ensuring you won't be disrupted by the telephone, find a quiet place to sit comfortably. Close your eyes, breathe rhythmically, and focus your imagination on a calm, inviting place, such as a tropical beach with the sounds of waves crashing or a meadow on a still day. Rest this way for a few minutes, and you'll feel more relaxed afterward.

At Home

I Can See Clearly Now

If you have a steady hand, you can save yourself a trip to the hairdresser and improve your line of sight by trimming your own bangs. The trick is to use small, sharp, pointed scissors—definitely not the large, blunt pair that has been quietly corroding in your desk drawer since 1990. In addition, snip your bangs when they are dry. Wet bangs will shrink as they dry, meaning you are likely to cut them too short if your hair is wet.

1. **Pin the hair you don't want to cut away from your face, so that you don't accidentally slay an innocent lock.**

2. **Run a fine-tooth comb through a bit of bang down to just above your intended length, and rest the comb against your brow to steady it.**

3. **Make little snips into small sections of hair below the comb teeth, upward at a 45-degree angle. Don't try to cut straight across unless you want to look like a 1930s farm boy.**

Face-framing, gamine-style bangs can be cut with a single-blade razor. Pull a little bit of your bang taut with your fingers and carefully use the razor to cut the hair at the intended length.

STEAM CLEAN **YOUR FACE**

Treat your face to an relaxing steam. Boil enough water to fill a large bowl half way. Add fresh or dried herbs, such as rosemary or lavender, to the water, if you like. Let the water cool just a bit, then drape a towel over your head and lean over the bowl, close enough to enjoy the steam but not close enough to scald yourself! Steam for a few minutes, then rinse your face in cool water and use a facial toner to clean away impurities loosened by steaming.

Debag Your Eyes

You really can soothe swollen, puffy eyes by taking a five-minute rest with cucumber slices placed over your eyes. Cucumbers contain the antiedemic compounds ascorbic acid and caffeic acid that help reduce swelling. They also have carotenoid, which is a chemical component of vitamin A. Often found in skin-care products, Vitamin A is absorbed through the skin and speeds the rate of cell turnover—thereby freshening your look!

WHY SUFFER FOR **BEAUTY?**

Plucking your eyebrows is one of those beauty tasks that's easy to put off, but if you have five minutes, arm yourself with tweezers and prepare to depilate! To reduce the pain and irritation, first soothe your nerve endings and open your pores with a washcloth wrung out in warm water pressed over the brow area. Pluck single hairs in the direction of growth with a single sharp tug. After plucking, soothe and disinfect the area with a pad soaked in a mild astringent, such as witch hazel or a skin toner for sensitive skin.

Renovate Your Lips

Fillers injected into the lips have been the rage among some celebrities for the past few years. However, there's a cheaper, less drastic, and easily reversed technique for achieving that popular bee-stung look—or, conversely, reducing lips that are a bit too pillowy:

- **Use a light concealer with an applicator to line your lips either just outside or inside your natural lip line. The concealer will effectively de-emphasize the true outline of your lips. Next use a sharpened, neutral-colored lip liner pencil to outline your lips, following the line of the concealer you have just applied.**

- **Fill in your lips in a quiet shade of gloss, using a lip brush instead of lipstick. It's better to use subtle shades and textures when you are trying to alter the natural lip line.**

Take a Micronap

Our productivity obsessed culture raises an eyebrow at midday napping; however, research supports the idea that brief naps—even for only five minutes, known as the micronap—have multiple benefits. A German study showed that micronappers had better recall of a list of memorized words than non-nappers. A five-minute micronap can also lower your heart rate, give your eyes a break, and let the crashing waves of your brain activity settle into a gentle swell.

Micronappers avoid the problem of feeling sluggish after a nap because they are unlikely to fall into REM sleep (the period in which we dream). The trick is not to fall deeply asleep—in five minutes you will probably remain peripherally aware of your surroundings. Sit back, close your eyes, breathe deeply and regularly, and let your mind drift. Many micro-nappers first take a 30-second introductory stretch, or will massage tense areas, such as the back of the neck.

CLEAN TEETH FOR A **HEALTHY HEART**

When you brush your teeth, spend a little extra time flossing and rinsing your mouth with an antibacterial mouthwash, and you can have a healthier cardiovascular system. Oral bacteria, particularly bacteria that move under the gums due to poor tooth or gum condition, have been linked to an increased risk of coronary artery disease, because inflammation-causing bacteria encourage plaque to form on arterial walls. People with periodontal disease have a doubled risk of coronary artery disease. There is no evidence that bacteria grows on your toothbrush, but the American Dental Association recommends replacing it every three to four months, or whenever the bristles are frayed.

STOMACH-SETTLING **GINGER TEA**

If for some reason you feel a bit queasy, try a five-minute antinausea remedy: a cup of fresh ginger tea. Chop a half teaspoonful of peeled fresh ginger, spoon into a mug, and steep in boiling water for three or four minutes. Strain and add some honey and lemon, if you like.

. . . .

Breast Cancer Check

It is a simple fact that every woman needs to clearly understand how to perform a breast self-examination to check for lumps that could be cancerous—and needs to do it every month. It helps if you become aware of the usual appearance and feel of your breasts, so you'll be more likely to notice any changes.

The best time to do an examination About a week after the start of your period, when your breasts will be less swollen and tender, is the best time of the month.

The exam Examine your breasts when you are relaxed and lying down. Use the sensitive pads of your fingertips, and follow an orderly pattern to palpate the entire breast, from armpit to cleavage and collarbone to rib. There are different examination patterns that you can use: spiraling in from the breast periphery to the nipple; up and down in rows as if you were mowing a lawn; or imagining the sphere of the breast as a pie divided into wedges and examining each wedge from the outer edge in to the nipple. Use a firm, circular motion to palpate all of the tissue. Feel for a lump, knot, thickening, or unusual heat, redness, or tenderness.

See your doctor right away if you notice Redness, distortion, visible swelling, puckering, dimpling, discharge from the nipple, or an inverted nipple.

The Statistics

If caught early, breast cancer is treatable. The stage 1 breast cancer survival rate is 100 percent, stage 2 is 92 percent, but by stage 4 it is only 20 percent.

At Home

Testicular Check

If you are a male 14 years of age or older, get into the routine of spending five minutes each month checking your testicles. Most conditions that affect the testicles are not serious, but there are just a few that can be. Being familiar with your testicles will help you to detect a problem early on, when it is easier to cure. Experts recommend that you do an examination after a warm bath or shower, because the heat from the water relaxes the scrotum (the skin that protects the testicles):

1. Standing in front of a mirror, examine the scrotum, looking for lumps on the skin or swellings inside.

2. Using both hands, with thumbs on top and index and middle fingers below, gently roll each testicle to examine it, then compare one with the other. It's normal for one testicle to be larger and lie lower than the other one.

3. Both testicles should be smooth except where the epididymis, the duct that carries sperm to the penis, runs. It is behind the testicle and feels bumpy.

Don't be alarmed if you find a lump. This is common and most lumps are benign (not a health risk). However, if you find a lump, make an appointment with your doctor or urologist right away. Testicular cancer is rare, but only a specialist can rule it out. Signs to watch out for:

- A lump in one testicle
- Pain or tenderness in either testicle or in the scrotum
- An unusual buildup of fluid inside the scrotum
- A heavy or dragging feeling in the groin or scrotum
- Enlarged or tender breasts (yes, this applies to males)
- A dull ache in either the groin or the lower abdomen
- An increase or reduction in size of a testicle (Remember, one testicle is usually larger than the other; however, the size and shape should remain much the same.)

GET RELIGION ABOUT **SUNSCREEN**

Dermatologists recommend that you apply sunscreen whenever you are outside for more than 10 minutes, even on overcast days, and reapply it every two hours or after sweating. Despite the benefits of sunscreen—shielding you from UVA rays (longer ultraviolet waves that age skin) and UVB rays (shorter waves that burn skin), both of which can cause serious skin cancers—it's a safe bet that sunscreen is not at the top of your to-do list. Make it a habit to spend five minutes slathering on the white stuff.

The American Academy of Dermatology recommends that adults use a sunscreen with a sun protection factor (SPF) of at least 15. An SPF of 15 deflects 93 percent of UVB rays; an SPF of 30 deflects 97 percent, which is recommended for sun-sensitive people. There are no standards for UVA rays, but look for broad-spectrum sunscreens that contain avobenzone, ecamsule, zinc oxide, or titanium dioxide. Apply sunscreen to all exposed areas of your body, including scalp, eyelids, hands, feet, neck, and ears. Use a lip balm that includes sunscreen.

At Home

....

Q: Do young people need to be concerned about getting skin cancer?

A: Yes. Skin cancer is the most common form of cancer in the United States, where 53,600 people each year develop melanoma, the most deadly type. The rate of squamous and basal cell carcinomas (both of which are common on skin areas exposed to the sun) in women under the age of 40 has tripled since the 1970s. As many as one in three teenage girls uses indoor tanning machines. Far from being healthy, a tan is the skin's injury response to excessive ultraviolet radiation.

Skin Cancer Check

No matter what type of skin you have, everyone needs to do a regular check for signs of skin cancer. You can either do it yourself, with the help of full-length and handheld mirrors, or you can enlist your partner to do the examination.

1. Start by examining the front and back of your body, then your left and right sides while you have your arms raised. If you are a woman, also check underneath your breasts.

2. Next bend your elbows and carefully examine your forearms, upper underarms, and the palms of your hands.

3. Check the backs of your legs and feet, including in between the toes and the soles of your feet. You may need to use the small mirror. Also use the mirror to check your back and buttocks, as well as the back of your neck and scalp—you may need to part your hair to see your scalp.

If you find any of the signs below, make an appointment with a dermatologist right away, and make sure that the person booking the appointment is aware of the nature of the visit. The earlier skin cancer is treated, the greater the chances are for a cure. Signs to watch out for include:

- Changes in the size, shape, color, or texture of a mark on your skin.

- A mole that is different from the rest.

- Any mole that itches, bleeds, or changes in any way.

- A sore that doesn't completely heal.

- A translucent growth that has rolled edges.

- A brown or black streak underneath a nail.

- A cluster of slow-growing, shiny pink or red lesions.

- A scar with a waxy feeling.

- A lesion that is flat or depressed and feels hard to the touch.

Have a Stretch

Exercise plays an important role in maintaining good health. For the best results, try to exercise for at least 30 minutes at a time. However, if you have only five minutes, use these simple stretches to help maintain your muscles, especially after you've been inactive for a length of time, such as after sitting for a long period or when you rise in the morning.

These gentle stretches can energize your joints and muscles—but make sure you don't overstretch. If you feel any pain, release the hold. Be sure to breathe deeply and fully while exercising. People often hold their breath without realizing it when they are concentrating.

Move!

Exercise keeps your muscles and bones strong, improves the efficiency of your lungs, and makes your body more flexible.

Single Arm Stretch

Stand with a good, centered posture, with your feet spaced equally apart and aligned with your shoulders and arms hanging straight down. Do not arch your back. Stretch one arm up to the ceiling while you stretch the other down and behind you—do not twist your body. Lower the arm and repeat with the opposite arm. Repeat this stretch 8–10 times.

Chest Stretch

Standing with a good centered posture (see above), extend your arms behind your back and interweave your fingers, palms toward you. Squeeze your shoulder blades together and raise your arms while holding your fingers clasped together. Hold this position for 20–30 seconds and release. Repeat this stretch 4–8 times.

At Home

. . . .

"Defer no time; delays have dangerous ends."

—William Shakespeare
English playwright (1564–1616

Standing Push-Ups

Five minutes of these easy push-ups will strengthen your arms, chest, and upper back.

Better Triceps

To work on your triceps in this position, bring your hands in closer, with arms parallel and in line with your shoulders.

1. Step about about 6 inches (15 cm) away from the wall, then turn to face the wall. Be sure your feet are in a stable, slip-free position (for example, avoid wearing socks on a very smooth floor surface) and are in hips' width apart.

2. Place your hands slightly wider than your shoulders' width against the wall, with arms straight but not locked at the elbow.

3. Slowly lower yourself (by bending at the elbow) as far toward the wall as you feel comfortable and can still maintain control, then straighten the elbows to push your upper body away from the wall and back to the starting position. Your feet need to remain in place. Do 8–10 repetitions.

The Push-Up—An All-Time Favorite

This is an easy version, and you can do as many as you want in five minutes.

1. Start on your hands and knees with your hands slightly wider than shoulders' width apart and with fingers forward.

2. Lower your hips toward the floor until you have a straight line from your head to your knees. Cross your ankles together.

3. Keeping your buttocks tight and your navel pulled toward your spine, slowly lower your chest to the floor without letting your body sag.

4. Go as far as you can while maintaining control, then raise your body up by straightening your elbows—do not lock them. Repeat 15–20 times.

Spinal Rotations

This exercise is designed to stretch and mobilize your spine and engages the oblique muscles of the abdomen.

1. Lie on your back, with your knees bent and feet parallel, hips' width apart. Place your arms out to the sides at shoulder height, resting on the floor, palms facing upward. Take a few moments to feel centered.

2. Now slowly let your legs roll sideways toward the floor, going as far as you feel comfortable. You may be able to go a little farther each time. Stay within your comfort zone while feeling a gentle stretch in your back and hips.

3. Return to the starting position, using your abdominal muscles as you do so. Repeat on the opposite side. Repeat 8–10 times in each direction.

Note If the above exercise is comfortable, you can add turning your head to the opposite side in which your legs are moving.

. . . .

Tummy Tightener

The aim here is to strengthen the abdominal muscles.

1. Lie on your back with your knees bent, feet flat on the floor, and arms by your side.

2. Tuck in your chin gently, leaving enough space for a tennis ball between your chin and breastbone.

3. Proceed by curling up, using your adominal muscles—do not let them bulge as you move. You can either hold your arms by your side or reach forward as you curl up.

4. Take a deep breath, relax, and then carefully uncurl in a slow and controlled movement.

Be aware You need to use your abdominal muscles for this exercise; try not to "hinge up" by using the muscles around your hips.

The Hundred

A popular Pilates exercise, the Hundred strengthens the abdominal muscles, improves the muscles that stabilize the shoulders, and warms up and energizes your body.

The Hundred is easier to learn in three stages. Before advancing to the later stages, you'll need to learn the Pilates method of breathing in stage one. Learning the correct breathing technique is important for achieving the best results in stages two and three. After you are comfortable doing the first stage, you can proceed to stage two—and you can even do all three stages if you feel confident. However, do not skip the first stage; you must build on each level.

Stage One: Breathing Exercise

1. Lie on your back with knees bent and feet flat on the floor. Place your hands on your rib cage and follow it down until you reach the lower torso. Start by becoming aware of your breathing pattern before beginning the exercise.

2. Progress to breathing in deep and wide, using your hands as a guide to where the expansion of your ribs needs to be, filling your sides and back for the count of 3 to 5 (whichever is more comfortable).

3. Breathe out, pulling your navel gently toward your back as you exhale to "hollow" for a count of 3 to 5.

Stage Two

1. Lie on your back with knees bent and feet flat on the floor. Extend your arms by your sides, palms facing down on the floor, and rest your head in line with your spine on the floor.

2. Engage your abdominal muscles and slowly, one at a time, bring your knees above your hips so you are in a chairlike posture, lying on the floor with your legs parallel. If this is too much, work on alternate legs until you are stronger. Do not arch your lower back.

3. Breathing as in the first stage (see opposite page), slowly raise your arms 4–6 inches (10–15 cm) off the floor. Make sure you keep your shoulder blades down and back, with your fingers reaching and lengthening.

4. Breathe out and pump your arms up and down in small, controlled movements for a count of 3 to 5. Repeat 8–10 times, then slowly return your feet to the floor one at a time.

Remember Do not let your back arch. Concentrate on your breathing pattern; do not overbreathe or hold your breath. If you become lightheaded during the exercise, this may be due to overbreathing. Return to stage one and breathe normally until you feel better. Once you feel better and feel that you can control your breathing, you can try stage two again.

Stage Three

This is the same as stages one and two, but this time, if you are ready for a more difficult level, make your head part of the exercise. By adding the head, you will help to strengthen the deep flexor muscles of your neck.

1. Lie on your back with knees bent and feet flat on the floor. Extend your arms by your sides, palms facing down on the floor, and rest your head in line with your spine on the floor.

2. As you raise your arms up 4–6 inches (10–15 cm), curl your neck and bring your head forward. Leave a space between your chin and breastbone. Continue in the chairlike position as in stage two, pumping your arms for a count of 3 to 5 in small, controlled movements before returning your feet to the floor.

Remember Once again, do not let your back arch and be sure to concentrate on your breathing pattern. Be aware of your head and neck position. Do not let your shoulders hunch up. Keep your chest open. If you begin to feel pain or tension increasing, return to stage two.

At Home

Renovate Your Resumé

In today's uncertain climate, it is important to have an impressive up-to-date resumé so you are fully prepared if a job opportunity arises. Employ your free five minutes to first review your resumé. Make sure it has accurate and current contact information, references, and accomplishments. Then use these suggestions to help make it stand out:

Make it snappy Effective resumés condense all but the most extensive careers to a single page. Human resource representatives will appreciate the time you've taken to make your resumé informative and to the point.

Organize by skill Chronological organization is not always the best method. Try using headings that highlight skills, such as "Project Leadership," "Product Development," or "Research."

Simplify the format Don't let the format get out of hand. Unusual fonts, colored paper, elaborate indents, and underlining are annoying, not professional.

Get it proofread Find someone skilled at grammar, punctuation, and spelling to proofread your resumé. A fresh set of eyes is far more likely to notice mistakes than yours if you've reviewed it a few times.

Avoid the "I" word Sentence fragments are acceptable in a resumé. Instead of "I taught five classes a semester and I developed a new freshman writing curriculum," it is better to state: "Developed innovative freshman writing curriculum while teaching five classes per semester."

Don't invent Putting the best face on your skills and accomplishments is fine, but untruths are unethical and are likely to be discovered in short order.

Be specific Provide a specific list of any specialized training that you possess, including foreign languages, computer programs, programming languages, or mechanical abilities.

KNOW YOUR **NUMBERS**

Make a list: Write down your bank and loan account numbers as well as credit card numbers, credit card expiration dates, customer service numbers, insurance policy numbers, and any other important information. Keep the list—and a duplicate—in two separate, secure locations. That way you'll have the necessary information if you ever lose your purse or wallet—or if you experience a home fire or robbery—and need to quickly contact the appropriate companies to make necessary changes to your account or to close it.

. . . .

SAY NO TO **TELEMARKETERS**

Tired of rushing to answer the ringing telephone, only to discover a telemarketer on the other end? The next time you're stuck in suspended animation for five minutes at home, call the National Do Not Call Registry at 1 (888) 382–1222. It will take you only about two minutes to register your phone numbers. Within 31 days of registration, telemarketers are legally obliged to cease calling you. If you have a computer, you can also register online at www.donotcall.gov.

. . . .

Q: How much junk mail do U.S. homes receive in a single day?

A: Enough fuel to heat 250,000 homes. Each year 5.6 million tons of catalogs and direct mail ads are added to landfills—that's about 100 million trees.

No More Junk Mail

For advice on removing your name from national mailing lists, send a letter plus a check for $1 to Mail Preference Service, Direct Marketing Association, P.O. Box 643, Carmel, NY 10512. To check this information or remove your name from other lists, visit www. privacyrights.org/fs/fs4-junk.htm, or do a search using "stop junk mail."

At Home

HALT **UNWANTED CATALOGS**

If you receive unwanted catalogs in your mail, you can stop the waste of paper by doing a search for "unwanted catalogs," or log onto www.catalogchoice.org and register for its free service. You can indicate which catalogs you don't want to receive, specify those that you do want, and the service will contact the retailers and make every effort to halt the unwanted mailings.

. . . .

CONSUMER ADVOCATE

Before making a purchase, search the Internet for reviews of the product. You might find manufacturers' reviews that can help you decide which model you want, or the reviews might be from consumers who pass on their experiences of using the product.

. . . .

Coupon Maven

Spend a few minutes searching the Internet for "discount coupons." Some sites, such as www.retailmenot.com and www.couponcabin.com, offer discount codes for online stores. Have another five minutes to spare? Sort out your paper coupons before you make a trip to a supermarket.

. . . .

WRITE IT DOWN

If you keep a journal, make an entry. You don't have to bare your soul in five minutes or be deep or insightful. Instead, be specific about the time of day, the details of who has just said what, the items in your line of sight—take down the photorealistic characteristics of your five minutes of freedom. Years from now, these plain and ordinary details will fascinate you.

> "One of the pleasures of reading old letters is the knowledge that they need no answer."
>
> —Lord Byron
> English poet (1788–1824)

Pen Your Own Haiku

Poems don't have to be epics—even the 14-line sonnet looks lengthy when compared to such abbreviated poetic forms as the Japanese haiku. An adaptation of an old poetic form, haiku are unrhymed, three-line poems of 17 syllables, in an arrangement of 5, 7, and 5 syllables per line. However, translations of Japanese haiku do not always conform to this syllabic arrangement because of the difficulties of translation, and there is no need for your five-minute effort to be syllabically irreproachable!

Traditionally, haiku are distillations of the little moments in nature or human interaction that tend to be quickly lost in the relentless rush of time—haiku puts a little crystal sphere around these moments. Surprisingly, haiku also have become a popular form to capture those vignettes of office life that everyone recognizes instantly. To get you started, here are two famous haiku to give you inspiration:

At Home

> Over the wintry
> Forest, winds howling in rage
> With no leaves to blow.
> (Muso Soseki, 1275–1351)

> The old pond
> A frog jumps in
> The sound of water.
> (Matsuo Basho, 1644–94)

Memorize a Poem

The American poet Emily Dickinson (1830–86) was a recluse, living her entire life in her father's house in Massachusetts, and in later life seldom left her bedroom. She carried on an intense epistolary communication with her publisher, Thomas Wentworth Higginson, and her sister-in-law, Sue Gilbert, until her death.

Dickinson wrote untitled poems that are punctuated by unconventional dashes and do not follow standard rhythmic structure. She had a genius for compressing the scant words but still providing powerful imagery. Dickinson's poems, due to their brevity, offer a unique opportunity to memorize some of the world's great literature in just five minutes.

There is another sky,
Ever serene and fair,
And there is another sunshine,
Though it be darkness there;
Never mind faded forests, Austin,
Never mind silent fields—
Here is a little forest,
Whose leaf is ever green;
Here is a brighter garden,
Where not a frost has been;
In its unfading flowers
I hear the bright bee hum:
Prithee, my brother,
Into my garden come!

I'm Nobody! Who are you?
Are you—Nobody—Too?
Then there's a pair of us?
Don't tell! They'd advertise—you know!
How dreary—to be—Somebody!
How public—like a Frog—
To tell one's name—the livelong June—
To an admiring Bog!

Limericks

Often used for nursery rhymes, limericks have been recited for centuries. They are five-line poems, following the rhyming pattern *aabba*: the first, second, and fifth lines (each of 7 to 10 syllables) rhyme, and the third and fourth lines (each of five to seven syllables) rhyme. One of the first known limericks is a prayer by St. Thomas Aquinas (1225–74). Here are some typical examples:

There was an old person of Hurst,
Who drank when he was not athirst;
When they said, "You'll grow fatter."
He answered, "What matter?"
That globular person of Hurst.
(Edward Lear, 1812–88)

There once was an old man of Lyme,
Who married three wives at a time.
When asked, "Why a third?"
He said, "One's absurd,
And bigamy, sir, is a crime."
(William Cosmo Monkhouse, 1840–1901)

There was a young lady named Laura
Who went to the wilds of Angora,
She came back on a goat
With a beautiful coat,
And notes of the fauna and flora.
(William Cosmo Monkhouse, 1840–1901)

A hungry young fellow named Perkins,
Was exceedingly fond of small gherkins,
One day before tea,
He ate forty-three,
And pickled his internal workin's!
(Unknown)

Aphorisms

Although they are not poems, aphorisms also focus a moment of perception into a pithy written form—usually just a sentence. Why not capture the accumulated wisdom of your years by creating your own five-minute aphorism? Here are examples of some famous ones to give you inspiration:

Lost time is never found again.
(Ben Franklin, 1706–90)

Believe nothing you hear,
and only half of what you see.
(Mark Twain, 1835–1910)

That which does not kill us makes us stronger.
(Freidrich Nietzche, 1844–1900)

All tyranny needs to gain a foothold is for
people of good conscience to remain silent.
(Thomas Jefferson, 1743–1826)

One should always play fairly when one has the
winning cards.
(Oscar Wilde, 1854–1900)

"Beauty is truth, truth beauty"—that is all
Ye know on earth, and all ye need to know.
(John Keats, 1795–1821, "Ode on a Grecian Urn")

The mind is its own place, and in itself
Can make a Heav'n of Hell, a Hell of Heav'n.
(John Milton, 1608–74, "Paradise Lost")

Education is a better safeguard of liberty
than a standing army.
(Edward Everett, 1794–1865)

Live as one already dead.
(Japanese proverb)

A rolling stone gathers no moss,
but it gains a certain polish.
(Oliver Herford, 1863–1935)

Swear Allegiance to Your Own Personally Composed Motto

While aphorisms could be described as wise words of advice, mottoes are words to live by in a concise sentence or phrase. Think for five minutes, and see if you can come up with a personal motto that seems right for you. Here are some examples of famous mottoes:

In God We Trust.
(National motto for the United States)

Out of many, one.
(Translated from *E Pluribus Unum,*
the motto carried by the American bald eagle
on the great seal of the United States)

Live free or die.
(State motto of New Hampshire)

While I breathe I hope.
(Translated from *Dum spiro spero,*
state motto of South Carolina)

Work conquers all things.
(Translated from *Labor omnia vincit,*
state motto of Oklahoma)

Always ready.
(Translated from *Semper Paratus,*
the U.S. Coast Guard motto)

Liberty, equality, brotherhood.
(Translated from *Liberté, egalité, fraternité,*
motto of the French Republic)

Swifter, higher, stronger.
(Translated from *Citius, Altius, Fortius,*
motto of the Olympics)

All the news that's fit to print.
(The *New York Times* motto)

Be prepared.
(Boy Scout motto)

At Home

GIVE YOUR BRAIN A WORKOUT WITH ANAGRAMS

From the Greek *ana*, meaning again, and *gramma*, or letter, combined to express "letters written anew," the object of an anagram is to take all of the letters in a word, name, or phrase, and create a new word, name, or phrase by using all of the letters available to you just once. Skilled anagrammatists can create new words, names, or phrases that are actual commentaries (often sardonic) on the original (or source) word or phrase. To get started, try making an anagram of your name.

. . . .

Constrained Writings

Anagrams are just one of several different types of wordplay disciplines known as "constrained writing," which must conform to some kind of arbitrary rule or pattern. These other examples will give the verbal sectors of your brain a good five-minute workout:

Lipogram Write sentences in which a letter, usually a common vowel, is forbidden, such as "e" in "Play a song on a piano."

Palindrome These are words that read the same backward and forward, such as "radar" or "tenet."

Semordnilap The word semordnilap is itself a palindrome of palindromes. A semordnilap is a word or phrase that spells a different word or phrase backward; some simple examples are pins/snip; diaper/repaid; live/evil; desserts/stressed.

Alliterative writing In either a phrase, sentence, or paragraph, every word must start with the same letter. For example, "the terrible truth told to the teacher troubled the theologist" is a phrase in which all words start with "t."

IVY LEAGUER ON YOUR OWN

Do you sometimes wish that you could go back to school, but don't have the time or money? Most of us wish that we had more opportunity to study—after all, intellectual curiosity does not shut down after formal schooling ends. The Massachusetts Institute of Technology is there to help. Through its website, MIT Open Courseware, the renowned university offers syllabi, lecture notes, assignments, and audio/video lectures for more than 90 percent of its courses—all free of cost. The courses are offered without credit, and, of course, no degree is earned. However, the meat of an MIT education is yours to begin downloading in five minutes. Visit the website http://ocw.mit.edu and begin scanning the extensive course offerings.

Globe Hop

When you listen to world news, do you realize that you have only a vague idea of the exact location of some of the world's countries? If you were asked to describe the location of Malawi, could you do better than "Africa"? Quick, where exactly is Uzbekistan? Five minutes with an atlas, globe, or on the Internet can settle these nagging questions for you, and set your mind off on a refreshing trip to exotic places, all without the need for passports, airline reservations, or luggage.

At Home

NEW WORLD CITIZENS

Take five minutes to ask adolescent or teenage children their opinion about an age-appropriate current event. It's a good idea to converse with kids about the world at large, not exclusively the life immediately around them. If you encourage your child to develop opinions in this way, you set the stage for a lifetime of engaged international citizenship.

HOME SCHOOL YOURSELF

The names of many African countries have changed in recent years, even with German East Africa being split into two different countries. The list below will help you catch up.

POST-COLONIAL NAME	COLONIAL NAME
Angola, Republic of	Portuguese West Africa
Benin, Republic of	Dahomey, Republic of
Botswana, Republic of	Bechuanaland Protectorate
Burkina Faso	Upper Volta
Burundi, Republic of	German East Africa/Ruanda-Urundi
Central African Republic	Ubangui-Shari
Congo, Democratic Republic of the	Zaire, Republic of
Congo, Republic of the	Middle Congo
Côte d'Ivoire, Republic of	Ivory Coast, The
Djibouti, Republic of	Afars and Issas, Territory of the
Equatorial Guinea, Republic of	Spanish Guinea
Ethiopia, Federal Democratic Republic of	Abyssinia
Ghana, Republic of	Gold Coast/ French West Africa
Guinea-Bissau, Republic of	Portuguese Guinea
Lesotho, Kingdom of	Basutoland, Territory of
Malawi, Republic of	Nyasaland Protectorate
Mali, Republic of	French Sudan
Namibia, Republic of	Southwest Africa
Rwanda, Republic of	German East Africa/Ruanda-Urundi
Somalia Republic	British Somaliland/Italian Somaliland
Tanzania, United Republic of	Zanzibar/Tanganyika
Uganda, Republic of	Buganda
Zambia, Republic of	Northern Rhodesia
Zimbabwe, Republic of	Southern Rhodesia

START ON THE ROAD
TO BECOMING A POLYGLOT

As you struggle with these simple phrases, consider the accomplishments of Ziad Youssef Fazah, a Lebanese (born in 1954) who is conversant in 58 languages!

LANGUAGE	HELLO	GOOD-BYE	DO YOU SPEAK ENGLISH
Apache	Ya' a'tay	Yadalanh	Ya' Nnaak' ehgo yánlti
Croatian	Zdravo or zhivio	Zbogom	Govorite li engleski?
Czech	Dobry den	Na shledanou	Mluvite anglicky?
Danish	God dag	Farvel	Taler De engelsk?
Farsi	Salaam	Khoda hafaz	Aya shoma Engalisi midanid?
French	Bonjour	Au revoir	Parlez-vous anglais?
German	Guten Tag	Auf Wiedersehen	Sprechen Sie Englisch?
Hindi	Namasté	Namasté	Kya apko angrezi ati hai?
Hungarian	Jó napot?	Viszlát	Beszél angolul?
Icelandic	Godan dag or hae	Bless	Talar pu ensku?
Italian	Ciao	Addio or Arrivederci	Parla inglese?
Japanese	Konnichiwa	Sayonara	Eigo o hanashimasu ka?
Mandarin Chinese	Ni hao	Zai jian	Ni hui jiang ying yu ma?
Norwegian	Goddág	Farvel	Snakker De engelsk?
Polish	Dzien dobry or witaj	Do widzenia or do zobaczenia	Czy mowisz po angielsku?
Portuguese	Como vai	Até a vista	Voce fala ingles?
Russian	Zdravstvuite	Dosvidanija	Vy govorite po-angliski?
Spanish	Hola	Adiós	Habla inglés?
Swedish	God dag	Hej da	Talar du engelska?
Tagalog	Kumustá?	Sige (informal)	Marunong ba kayong mag Ingles?
Turkish	Merhaba	Allaha ismarladik	Ingilizce konusur musunuz?
Urdu	Salaam aleekum	Khuda hafiz	Aap Angraizi boltay hain?

At Home

CHAPTER FOUR

In the Car

The time you spend in a car presents unlimited opportunities to improve your life with the resourceful five-minute solutions offered in this chapter. And, too, there's something about being alone in a car that gives you time to think. Safety is important, so make sure you don't do anything that will interfere with the flow of traffic. In fact, some of these suggestions are best done while waiting to pick up someone.

RETUNE **THE RADIO**

Why not tune into a radio station that you've never listened to before? Expand your musical tastes—try a type of music that you don't know well—or adjust the radio to a station that broadcasts news events or audio plays of fictional stories.

LEARN A **NEW LANGUAGE**

Listen to a foreign-language radio station to teach yourself the language. This will be most useful if you are studying the language and have an idea of its grammar and vocabulary. But even if you're a neophyte, you can begin to get a sense for the language's rhythms and intonations. By listening for a few minutes every day, you will be able to pick out some recurring words and phrases, and then later look up the words in a dual-language dictionary.

Make a List of Songs about Cars

The list of songs about cars is longer than a line of cars waiting to cross New York's George Washington Bridge at rush hour! Here are some classics to get you thinking:

- **Little Deuce Coupe (The Beach Boys)**
- **Drive My Car (The Beatles)**
- **Fast Car (Tracy Chapman)**
- **Oh Lord Won't You Buy Me a Mercedes Benz (Janis Joplin)**
- **Dead Man's Curve (Jan and Dean)**
- **Cars (Gary Numan)**
- **Mustang Sally (Wilson Pickett)**
- **Little Red Corvette (Prince)**
- **Hey Little Cobra (The Rip Chords)**
- **Red Barchetta (Rush)**
- **My Hooptie (Sir Mix-A-Lot)**

Improve Your Singing Voice

The windows are up and no one can hear you, so now is the time to experiment with your voice. Are you an operatic soprano, folksy crooner, or Broadway belter? Whatever your preferred style, you can warble your way to a better vocal technique in the sealed rehearsal chamber of your car.

If no one is listening, you'll relax, which will let loose any vocal abilities you have. Vary your volume until you find what is natural for you. Overloud singing can cause your voice to go flat. Singing too softly—such as when you don't want others to hear—hinders you from developing the natural tone of your voice. Once you've found your best volume, practice singing at different pitches. The idea is to exercise your vocal muscles and get to know your capabilities. Here are some suggestions:

- **Find your own tone.** Tone is the characteristic sound of a voice. Attractive singing voices can vary widely in tone: Compare the rich velvety sound of a crooner to the nasal twang of a folkie.

- **Practice singing with an "open throat."** Raise your soft palate to amplify the tone quality of your voice. To do this, imagine the way your throat feels at the beginning of a yawn.

- **Find your natural range.** Experiment with the different vocal ranges (bass, baritone, tenor, alto, mezzo-soprano, and soprano).

- **Sing vowel sounds.** This teaches you to move your mouth to create the different sounds. One easy way to sing vowel sounds is to imitate animal vocalizations that you know well, such as the moo of a cow or baa of a sheep!

- **Practice scales and arpeggios.** Sing up and down the scale to increase the agility of your voice.

In the Car

Spiff Up Your Speech

If you think that the discipline of elocution (the art of public speaking) is old-fashioned, consider how much attention is paid to presidential debates, or how certain teachers are considered "stars" because their speaking style grabs their students' attention. Verbal tics, such as the tendency to speak all sentences as though they were questions, or sloppy diction, such as slurring words, can destroy the impact of even the most potent talking points.

Articulation, or pronouncing words clearly and correctly, is central to elocution. Besides precise diction, you can vary your tone of voice, change the speed at which you speak, and place a variety of accents on the words in a sentence to subtly change their meaning. While you're in the car, put your articulation skills through their paces by practicing some tongue twisters. Take your pick from this list of exercises to get you started:

B sounds

Betty bought a bit of butter,
but she found the butter bitter,
so Betty bought a bit of better butter
to make the bitter butter better.

D sounds

Did Doug dig Dick's garden or did Dick dig
Doug's garden?

F sounds

Four furious friends fought for the phone.

G sounds

The great Greek grape growers grow great
Greek grapes.

H sounds

How was Harry hastened so hurriedly from the hunt?

L sounds

Larry sent the latter a letter later.

Lucy lingered, looking longingly for her lost lapdog.

N (and U) sounds

You know New York,
You need New York,
You know you need unique New York.

P sounds

Peter Piper picked a peck of pickled peppers.
If Peter Piper picked a peck of pickled peppers,
where's the peck of pickled peppers that Peter
Piper picked?

Q sounds

Quick kiss. Quicker kiss. Quickest kiss.

R sounds

Round the rugged rocks the ragged rascal ran.

Reading and writing are richly rewarding.

S sounds

The shrewd shrew sold Sarah seven silver fish slices.

Sister Susie sat on the seashore sewing shirts
for sailors.

T sounds

Ten tame tadpoles tucked tightly in a thin tall tin.

Two toads totally tired, trying to trot to Tewkesbury.

V sounds

Vincent vowed vengeance very vehemently.

Vera valued the valley violets.

In the Car

Roar Like a Lion

It's not practical to practice a full yoga posture in a car, but you can adapt one traditional pose, the *simha asana*, or lion pose, to help exercise your face and jaw muscles. However, make sure that the car is not in motion while you do this exercise:

1. While sitting behind the wheel, place the heels of your hands on your knees and straighten your arms. Keep your back and head erect.

2. Inhale as you lean forward slightly, and at the same time stretch your fingers from your knees.

3. Open your jaws as wide as you can. Stick out your tongue, stretching it down as far as possible. At the same time, focus your eyes on your nose. Hold this position as you breathe in for 30–60 seconds.

4. Now exhale, releasing your forward stretch, relaxing your fingers on your knees, and closing your mouth and eyes. Repeat 3 to 5 times.

If you want to also stimulate your throat, roar loudly like a lion as you stick out your tongue!

. . . .

What's the Fashion

If you're stuck in traffic in a big city, use your ringside seat to observe the free fashion show that will be strutting along the sidewalks. Street fashion is often far ahead of designers and fashion magazines, whose "revolutionary" ideas are often adapted from their observations of the latest styles in urban neighborhoods.

ROAD **DIARY**

Tired of waiting in the car for someone who is persistently late? Keep a large sketch pad or journal in the car, along with some pens and colored pencils. Instead of fidgeting when there is time to kill, make a quick entry or sketch. If your journey to your meeting destination was not the most pleasant one, this would be a good way to vent some anger. At the end of the year, you will have your own personal Road Warrior Diary.

Plot a Novel

As you sit in your car, jot down some details about the people around you in a notebook to describe their appearance and behavior. Imagine where they might be going or what they might be about to do. Use this information to form an outline of a story. You'll be surprised by how much you can invent in five minutes—and you just might have the beginnings of a best-selling novel!

"We are all travelers in the wilderness of this world, and the best we can find in our travels is an honest friend."

—Robert Louis Stevenson
Scottish author (1850–94)

Q: If you are stopped in traffic, is it better to turn off the engine?

A: Not if you'll be stopped for five minutes or less. You will burn more gas restarting the car than you will idling for five. However, once you're heading toward a 10-minute or longer wait, it's more fuel efficient to turn off the engine.

In the Car

Write Mental Traffic Tickets

You may not have the flashing red-and-blue lights, the hat, shades, and the official book of traffic tickets. However, you can still scan the roads for lawlessness. See how many flagrant violations you can spot. Here are a few traffic transgressions to keep an eye out for:

- Following too closely. Cars need to follow the "three-second" rule (see below).

- Signaling sins: Not using turn signals, or not using them at least three seconds before a turn. Not signaling before making a lane change.

- Speeding up when another vehicle is trying to pass.

- Passing on a nonpassing stretch of road (solid instead of dotted-line lane dividers).

- Traveling in the passing lane.

- A slow vehicle not traveling in the far right lane.

- Failure to come to a complete stop at a stop sign.

- Speeding up instead of slowing down for a yellow traffic light.

- Turning right at a red light when a sign prohibits it.

- Failure to yield the right of way to traffic already in the intersection.

- Failure to yield to pedestrians in a crosswalk.

- Failure to use headlights from half an hour after sunset to half an hour before sunrise, or if visibility is not clear for at least 1,000 feet (300 m) ahead.

....

THREE **ONE-THOUSAND**

To make sure there's enough room between you and the car in front of you, choose a landmark on the road ahead. As the vehicle in front of you passes it, count "one-one thousand, two-one thousand, three one-thousand." If you pass the landmark before you've finished saying "three one-thousand," you need to increase the distance between you and the car ahead of you.

Q: When do most animal and vehicle collisions occur?

A: In the hours between dusk and dawn, especially in areas that tend to attract wildlife, such as roads near fields with forage or close to water sources. If you are driving in these conditions, slow down and be alert. May to October are high-risk months for deer, September to October for bear, and, in the far northern United States and Canada, December to January for moose. Watch for eyes shining when hit by headlights, and if you see one animal, expect another. Use your horn or flash your lights, but be aware: animals act unpredictably.

. . . .

ZERO TOLERANCE FOR DROWSY DRIVERS

Five minutes is not enough time to emphasize the importance of staying awake while driving. The U.S. National Highway Traffic Safety Administration estimates that drowsy drivers cause an average of 100,000 highway crashes each year. If you find yourself yawning and with an intense desire to close your eyes while driving, it is important to know that the traditional subterfuges—opening the windows, blasting the radio, slapping your own face, or drinking coffee—will not be enough to keep you awake. If you are sleep deprived, there is no substitute for sleep and no excuse for continuing to drive while drowsy. It's simply too dangerous—if you nod off, or even let your eyes close for a mere five seconds, you have driven your car blind for about 100 yards (90 m) and you risk an accident.

On a long, monotonous trip, take 15-minute breaks every two hours or 100 miles (160 km). Take five minutes before you get started to look at a road map and plan your breaks, such as at rest areas or where you can pull off a highway at an exit. When you take a break, take a few minutes to walk or jog in fresh air. Eating high-protein snacks will maintain your blood-sugar level, but do not overeat; "stuffing" induces the urge for a siesta.

What Kind of Road Is It?

The next time you're stuck in traffic, take five minutes to mull over the precise definition of the paved way that entraps you. If you're confused as to precisely which kind of road you are traveling on, you're not alone. A highway is a general term for a variety of main roads. Although the Department of Transportation's *Manual on Uniform Traffic Control Devices* makes specific distinctions between a freeway and an expressway, in practice, individual states continue to define roads idiosyncratically. The distinctions are as follows:

- **Freeway** A divided highway with full access control. Access to freeways is allowed only at interchanges.

- **Expressway** A divided highway with partial access control. It may have a limited number of private driveways and intersections.

- **Parkway** Usually older roads (from the 1930s–50s) with limited access. Trucks are not allowed, and they have wide, wooded, or parklike right of ways.

- **Turnpike** Open to cars, trucks, and buses, but there is a toll. Turnpike is a term that dates to the fifteenth century. Pikes were wooden barriers first used to prevent access to a road to reduce the likelihood of attack by highwaymen. Later, pikes were used to block roads until a toll was paid, at which point they were turned aside. Today, turnpikes are still toll roads—but the pikes are remote controlled!

- **Frontage road** A nonlimited-access road that runs parallel to a higher speed road, usually a freeway, and feeds it at points of access (interchanges). In many cases, the frontage road was already in existence when the limited-access road was built.

- **Interstate** This can incorporate expressways and freeways. As the name implies, an interstate highway is part of the federal system of highways that connects many states. Even numbers go east and west; odd numbers run north and south.

Q: Which city has the highest traffic delay per driver?

A: Statistics vary, but they all agree that Los Angeles is the worst. One report claims that drivers in the city spent an average of 72 extra hours stuck in traffic in 2005.

. . . .

Weary O' the Road

The next time you are stuck in traffic and have had enough of modern travel in general, take comfort in this romantic-era renunciation of the urge to take to the road. It was written by world traveler and poet Lord Byron when he was only 29 (and already weary of traveling).

> So, we'll go no more a roving
> So late into the night,
> Though the heart be still as loving,
> And the moon be still as bright.
> For the sword outwears its sheath,
> And the soul wears out the breast,
> And the heart must pause to breathe,
> And love itself have rest.
> Though the night was made for loving,
> And the day returns too soon,
> Yet we'll go no more a roving
> By the light of the moon.

. . . .

BE PREPARED FOR **AN EMERGENCY**

No one plans to be stranded in a car during a breakdown or snowstorm that can last for hours. Take five minutes to make sure you have the following in the glove compartment or trunk of your car: flashlight (the windup type that won't have dead batteries), multifunctional tool (the kind with a bottle opener, file, pliers, screwdriver, and blade can be handy in an emergency), a spare tire, first-aid kit, space blanket, flares, and freeze-dried food. And it's always wise to bring along a bottle of water.

The Fuel Filter

If you notice that your car seems listless, lacks energy, is slow to pick up, and hesitates, these are signs that the fuel filter may need replacing.

SOLEMNLY SWEAR TO YOUR DASHBOARD...

That you will give it the respect that it deserves. First, use a microfiber cloth—or failing that, a tissue—to dust it off so that your dashboard will shine forth. Then make your oath, with an extra special vow never to put duct tape over the check engine light (see opposite page) and to pay attention to what the various gauges are trying to tell you!

YOUR DASHBOARD IN **ANCIENT GREEK**

Did you know that some of the gauges on your dashboard have a Greek connection? The tachometer, the gauge that measures the rate of rotation of the engine's crankshaft in revolutions per minute (rpm), takes its name from *tachos*, the Greek word for speed, combined with *metron*, or to measure. If the tachometer in your car reads 1, 2, or 3, it is referring to 1,000, 2,000, or 3,000 revolutions per minute. Revving your engine so that the tachometer ascends into the red zone will damage the engine. If you're driving a manual-transmission car, try not to linger in the low gears: the lower the gear, the higher the rpm, the greater the workload on the engine, and the more fuel you use. The ideal situation is to shift into the highest gear possible at the lowest speed, but you will sacrifice acceleration.

Odometer is derived from the Greek *hodos*, meaning path or way—an obsolete name for odometer is hodometer. The odometer measures your mileage. The word mile also has an ancient link. It comes from the Latin *mille passum*, which means a thousand paces, where a pace equaled two steps of a Roman foot soldier.

The Gauge That Gets No Respect: The Check-Engine Light

Tales abound of risk takers who drive their cars for months with the plaintive glow of the check-engine light a not-so-comforting constant on their dashboards. What is this light trying to tell you? Usually, it's related to the car's emissions system.

In modern cars, the check-engine light is part of the car's onboard-computer diagnostic system that samples emissions before they enter the catalytic converter and again as they exit the tailpipe. If you're lucky, the check-engine light is telling you to tighten your gas cap; on the other hand, your catalytic converter could need replacing. Almost certainly, you are driving a nonemissions-compliant vehicle. Luckily, the same in-car computer that fired up your light has also stored a trouble code that can be read by the diagnostic computer in any modern automotive repair center.

Take five minutes to make sure the gas cap is tight. If that doesn't work, it's time to visit your auto mechanic. On some car models, the light will glow at first to give you a warning, but flash when you need to get the car to a mechanic quickly. Check your manual, but if you're not sure, don't delay.

. . . .

THE **FUEL GAUGE**

Although it's true that most gauges allow for a couple of gallons of fuel in reserve even when reading empty, playing a game of chicken with the fuel gauge will probably shorten the life of your fuel pump. The fuel pump is designed to run submerged in gas. A low gas level forces the pump to work harder to pump the little gas that's left, while removing its source of cooling, thus shortening its life. Spend a few minutes refilling the gas tank.

Q: Does anybody keep gloves in the glove compartment?

A: Perhaps. In the early days of driving, when cars were open, uninsulated, and unheated, glove compartments were for gloves—vital to keep your hands in workable, unfrozen condition. Nowadays, the glove compartment could be more accurately described as the document compartment, because it is most often used to hold the papers associated with the car, such as insurance cards, a registration, and maps.

....

Glove Compartment Archaeology

The next time you're waiting in the car, turn your attention to the glove compartment. What's in there anyway? Have you ever dug down deep into the strata? Arm yourself with a bag for trash and prepare to excavate the layers.

- **Required** Proof of insurance. Driving without your current insurance card (not one expired two years ago) is a surefire way to find yourself featured in the police log of your local paper.

- **Required, probably** Current registration. Some recommend that you keep the car registration in your wallet instead of the glove compartment, because the registration can make it easier for a thief to sell your car.

- **Handy to have** Sanitary hand wipes (if they are contained in a sealed package), pen and paper (if the pen is capped and functional), tire gauge, duct tape (to fix your side-view mirror), sunglasses, and sunscreen.

- **Definitely trash** Old receipts, expired parking passes or coupons, maps about to disintegrate, elderly or grimy packages of food condiments, burned-out batteries, scratched CDs, old lipsticks, and grungy combs.

Get a Wide-Screen View

If you're stopped on a highway with cars backed up in front of you, as well as behind you and on both sides, and there's no chance you'll be moving in the next five minutes, you can check that your side-view mirrors are adjusted so there are no gaping blind spots in your rear view. Of course, this is much better to do before you leave your home:

- First ensure your rear-view mirror is adjusted so that a car squarely behind you appears in the center of the mirror.

- To set the left side-view mirror: Lean all the way to the left so that your head touches the closed window, then adjust the left-side mirror out until you can just barely see the left back corner of your car at the inside edge of your left side-view mirror.

- To set the right side-view mirror, from the driver's seat: Lean your head to the right as much as possible, then adjust your right side-view mirror out until you can just barely see the right back corner of your car at the inside edge of your right side-view mirror.

If your mirrors are correctly adjusted, as soon as the left front headlight of a car behind you disappears from your rear-view mirror, it will appear in your left side-view mirror—seamlessly, without delay. The same needs to be true of the right side—as a right headlight disappears from your rear mirror, it will be showing up in your right side-view mirror.

In the Car

. . . .

"One always begins to forgive a place as soon as it's left behind."

—Charles Dickens
English novelist (1812–70)

 137

Check Your Tire Pressure

For safety and good gas mileage, it is important to have your tires at the right pressure. Check your tire pressure at least once a month. However, be sure to do it more often if it's been very hot or cold. Tires are higher in pressure when hot and lose pressure when cold.

1. Check your tire pressure when the tires are cold, before you start to drive. Unscrew the valve cap.

2. Press a tire gauge firmly onto the valve. If you hear escaping air, you are pressing too lightly or crookedly. Read the gauge. You can find the correct pressure for your tires on a plate inside the car's driver-side door, or in your owner's manual.

3. If necessary, add a little air, and then check again. If you are nervous about adding air, ask someone at your local gas station to show you how. Add a little at a time, then recheck the pressure.

. . . .

Is Your Car Crying Out for Help?

You may have missed your car's cries for help by singing loudly or listening to the radio. Make sure you have a few quiet minutes as you drive to really listen to your car. If you notice any of the following noises, it's time for a visit to a car mechanic:

- **Hissing** Hose leak

- **Backfire** Ignition timing off, leaky valves

- **Engine clatter** Low on engine oil, poorly adjusted or leaky valves

- **Engine knock that increases as you drive** Worn camshaft or cam followers

- **Screeches on acceleration** Loose or slipping fan belt

- **Screeches when turning** Power-steering belt may need adjusting

- **Squealing brake** Have the pads and rotors checked as soon as possible

CAN YOUR CAR **DRIVE STRAIGHT?**

If you're in slow traffic, you can test the front-end alignment of your car to see if it can drive in a straight line. Rest your hands lightly on the steering wheel—so you are ready to tighten in a flash, if necessary—and accelerate slightly with the car pointed in a straight line. The car needs to continue in a straight line without drifting to either side. If the car pulls or wanders, check the tire pressure (see page 138). If the tire pressure is OK, make an appointment with a mechanic to check the front-end alignment.

What's That Smell?

If you are waiting in traffic, have a good sniff. Is there a funny smell? If your car gives off any of these odors, it might be time to book an appointment at the local garage:

- **Maple syrup** Leaking coolant (toxic ethylene glycol), possibly from a failed intake manifold or cylinder head, a bad heater core, leaky radiator, or missing radiator cap

- **Gym locker room** Mold growing in the car. (Did you leave the windows or sunroof open when it rained?) Or mildew could be growing in the A/C evaporator

- **Gasoline** Missing gas cap, leaky fuel injection line, or fuel tank vent hose

- **Rotten eggs** Hydrogen sulfide, possibly a fuel injection or catalytic converter problem

- **Brimstone, otherwise known as sulfur** Leaking from the manual transmission, transfer case, or differential housing

- **Hot oil** Leak in the engine, causing oil to drip and burn on the hot exhaust manifold

- **Burned carpet** Overheated brake pads, possibly caused by a stuck brake caliper piston

- **Burned paper** The clutch facing is burning on a slipping clutch

In the Car

A Comfortable Seat

The next time you need to wait for someone in your car, take five minutes to make sure you're sitting comfortably at the driver's seat. To help you adjust the seat to the correct position, follow these suggestions:

- To make sure you have maximum road visibility, raise your seat as high as it is comfortable for you—but be sure that you have adequate head clearance from the roof. You don't want to hit your head on it when on a bumpy road.

- Now move the seat forward until you can completely and comfortably engage the gas pedal and brake, then adjust the seat height for good pedal control, if necessary.

- Adjust the angle of the seat's cushion tilt to provide support for your thighs along the length of the cushion, making sure you avoid any pressure behind the knees.

- Next adjust the backrest to ensure even support along your back. Make sure you avoid reclining the seat too far back, because this may cause you to compensate by leaning your head and neck forward, which would put unnecessary pressure on your neck muscles.

- Set the steering wheel toward you and downward for easy reach. However, make sure there is adequate clearance for your legs and that you can still see the dashboard clearly.

- Adjust the headrest to support your head and neck in line with your spine.

Note Seat adjustments vary between car models—check your owner's manual to familiarize yourself with your own car's features.

Lower Back Strengthener

This is a great exercise for improving the muscles in the lower back area while you are sitting, and what better time than while you're sitting in a car? It also helps to develop better postural awareness.

Stretch Your Legs

If you are waiting in a parking lot, get out of the car and take a walk around it. Parking lots aren't often beautiful, but it is a good time to stretch your legs.

1. While sitting in your seat with your feet flat on the floor, let your back and shoulders slump. Tighten your buttocks; as you squeeze them together, you will feel yourself rising slightly in your chair.

2. Maintain the contraction in your buttocks and start to lift from your chest, using the muscles alongside your spine to help you reach a taller sitting posture. Hold for 10–15 seconds and repeat.

Ankle Circles

These are good for circulation and maintaining a good range of movement in your ankle joints.

1. Circle your foot slowly and fully in either direction. Make sure the movement is from the ankle joint, not just wiggling toes or rolling your leg.

2. Perform 6–8 circles in one direction, then reverse the circle direction. Repeat with the opposite leg.

Shoulder Rolls

After holding the steering wheel for what may seem like hours, take a few minutes' break to do this exercise.

1. Sit in your seat, with your back supported, arms relaxed by your side, and head still and centered.

2. Slowly pull your shoulders up to your ears. Then squeeze your shoulder blades back and together; relax and let your shoulders drop. Repeat 8 times, then reverse, pulling your shoulder blades forward.

In the Car

CHAPTER FIVE

In Line

When waiting in line, you may often feel as if you're simply a link in a long chain—one of many who provide fodder to marketers and psychologists—those folks who hope you don't snap and break the chain! Although you may feel trapped, you can change your experience to one that offers opportunities for social interaction. Set a good example for your fellow "links" by smiling instead of scowling and maybe offering a helping hand or a healing remark. Alternatively, follow some of these suggestions for amusing yourself as the line diminishes at a snail's pace in front of you.

START A **CONVERSATION**

Lines can get tense when people who are waiting lose a sense of perspective about their plight. Bring the situation back to Earth by making a witty comment. If it raises a smile, you might even consider starting a conversation. Safe topics include comments on the store sales, how crowded the parking lot is, the store's new renovation—or need for a renovation. Ask the person next to you if he or she has ever tried the in-store bank or pharmacy, or if that person knows a good recipe using something you've bought, such as a particular vegetable or cut of meat. If you are waiting in a clothes store, ask your neighbor's opinion of a new clothing style sold in the store. If you're at an airport, mention your destination to your neighbor, and ask if he or she has ever been there—it will seem less intrusive than asking where they are headed.

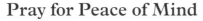

Pray for Peace of Mind

The objects of desire we are willing to wait in line for are usually secular, if not prosaic: a car registration, a cell phone, a bag of groceries. If you're feeling beaten down by the banality of it all, take heart from the thought that the pure, sacred act of prayer is yours in an instant.

The act of prayer—the word is derived from the Old French *prier*, meaning "to plead, beg, or ask earnestly"—is common to every religion, although the forms prayer can take vary widely. Some modern people who revere prayer believe that it is not necessarily a supplication—sometimes it's just opening yourself to the presence of your own personal God. There is something lovely in the thought that while doing something physical, such as standing in line to pay a parking ticket, you can spiritually be finding peace in the divine.

MAKE A LIST OF YOUR PERSONAL HEROES

Waiting in line is a good time to reflect on issues, whether simply thinking about plans for the following day or something more retrospective. Have you ever stopped to think about the people you truly admire in life? These are the individuals who make you feel better just by thinking about them and have accomplished something you deeply, honestly respect. Our true personal heroes tend to be people who have not merely accomplished something great. Perhaps they are our heroes because we can think of them in a crisis and take comfort from the mere fact that they've existed. Take five minutes and put together your personal hero list. Your list will reveal a lot about you as a person and the qualities that you most value.

Patron Saint of the Line

If you see someone struggling to find a ringing cell phone or write something down while holding a lot of packages, offer to hold the packages for a moment.

....

WRITE YOUR OWN TEN COMMANDMENTS

If you've already memorized the traditional Christian Ten Commandments, now is the time to do your own personal version. You might find that your own ten commandments will reveal a lot about your past personal experiences, which have hopefully taught you some lessons about how to behave appropriately. You might have to dig deep, and you'll probably find yourself rephrasing your commandments and rearranging them in order of priority.

Sometimes personal commandments can suggest more than they actually say, for example, the hypothetical commandment "Remember that you are mortal" would influence a whole host of behaviors, from how you pay attention to your regular health care to how you embrace risks, depending on the interpretation of the commandment! The commandments that you devise might not be as specific as "Do not steal," but having your own personal ten commandments to hold close to your heart can be a real comfort in times of trial or tribulation.

In Line

SETTLE BACK **IN YOUR MIND**

How many times have you complained, "I never have any free time"? When waiting in line you're not physically free—if you move too far, you might lose your place—and sometimes it can seem like your mind and spirit come to a halt as you wait. You are in a state called "in abeyance," from the Old French *abaer*, meaning "to expect or wait." You can use this little time warp to be quietly aware of life around you—to look, to appreciate whatever is there, or not there. If you don't want to observe what is around you, allow yourself some quiet time, perhaps placing yourself on a warm, sandy beach or relaxing on a sailboat.

. . . .

Tidy Up Your Appearance

As long as you don't infringe on those around you, pay attention to your appearance while you wait, especially if you want to impress the person whom you are waiting for, such as a bank manager. If you carry a large handbag or a briefcase with you, consider including a package of sanitary hand wipes as part of your essentials:

- Take off your coat and give it a good shake and brush it off to remove dust and lint.

- Polish your eyeglasses with a lens-cleaning tissue.

- Use a hand wipe to remove dried-on dirt on your shoes, and discreetly fold it up and pocket it if a trash can is not available.

- Remove any items in your pockets that will make your clothing appear bumpy, such as the earring that has been missing for the last few weeks.

Consider a Makeover

Use your time in line to note the new fashion trends being modeled among the captive audience waiting in line with you. From head to toe, you'll find an amazing array of styles. How someone else puts an outfit together is a great way to get inspiration, even if you pick up only certain elements from the complete look. Don't forget the accessories: A plain dress or shirt can be made more interesting by adding the right belt, scarf, or jewelry. Of course, be discreet in your observations because obvious staring will make others feel uncomfortable.

Name That Accent

Test your accent IQ by seeing how many accents you can identify in the voices around you.

> "All human wisdom is summed up in two words—wait and hope."
> —Alexandre Dumas
> French writer (1802–70)

MAKE A DATE IN **YOUR CALENDAR**

If you have either a personal organizer or a cell phone with a calendar feature, use it to help keep track of dates that are important to you, such as birthdays and anniversaries of family and friends. Make sure you also use it to help remind you of upcoming events, including presentations, doctor's or dentist's appointments, school performances, and, of course, wedding and graduation dates. While in line, take the time to check these dates for the upcoming weeks—you might just discover that you've forgotten to pick up a birthday card that needs mailing to someone special!

In Line

TAKE A LOOK AT A PHONE OR UTILITY BILL

Make an Appointment

A brief phone call to make an appointment is not as annoying to others as a long conversation in public—but you run the risk of being "in line" and "on hold" at the same time.

If you have a recent bill from your cell phone, landline phone, gas or oil, electricity, cable, or Internet provider in your purse or briefcase, take the time while you are waiting in line to give the statement a good hard inspection. Most bills today are broken down into a long list of fees for services, some that you might not be using (such as ringtone downloads or phone replacement insurance on a cell-phone bill), others that you might not even recognize. Ask yourself if the itemized charges seem valid, if the services described are ones that you truly need, and if there is anything that you think is either inaccurate or expendable. Put a check mark next to anything on the bill that seems questionable, and call customer service with a query when you have another five minutes in a more private place.

....

Q: Which is correct, the term "in line" or "on line"?

A: According to most dictionaries of standard English usage, "in line" is the correct expression. However, "on line" is a regional variation in New York City and its vicinity that has started to appear in other regions of the country.

"Everything in life that we really accept undergoes a change."

—Katherine Mansfield
New Zealand writer
(1888–1923)

Collate Your Coupons

If you have an envelope full of coupons that you plan on using, check them to be sure that they are not expired and that your purchase fulfills the conditions of the coupon. If you have a coupon or two that you can't use (maybe you have two and the coupon says "one per customer"), make a friendly gesture and offer the extra one to someone next to you in line.

. . . .

WHICH IS **BETTER VALUE?**

If you're standing in line at a store, calculate the unit price of some of the items you are just about to purchase. To find the unit price, divide the cost of the item by the number of units. If you bought a package of socks—6 pairs for $8.99—how much did each individual sock (a single unit) cost?

$8.99 \div 12 = 75$ cents per individual sock (rounded off)

Calculating the unit price is most useful when deciding which package size is least expensive. For example, a 1 pound (450 g) can of coffee may cost just $5.99, while a 3 pound (1.36 kg) can is $10.00. However, the unit price breaks down to 37 cents per pound for the 1 pound (450 g) can and just 21 cents per pound for the 3 pound (1.36 kg) can.

. . . .

Uncrumple Your Cash

Count the money in your wallet, and arrange the bills neatly so that all of the denominations are together and the bills all face the same way. This will make it easier for you to pay for your items when you finally reach the cashier.

Total the Damage

If you have a cart full of items at a store, try adding their total cost in your head. If you're mathematically challenged, you can reach a good estimate by rounding off the price of each item to the nearest whole number (for example, count $3.69 as $4.00, but $2.25 as $2) and adding the whole numbers.

NUTRITION BATTLE OF THE **LABELS**

Take one of your favorite snacks, such as a candy bar from a nearby display, and read the ingredient list, number of calories, and grams of fat. Compare your favorite to its competition. Maybe you can find a somewhat healthier alternative. However, be warned—low-fat items are often loaded with sugar.

VACATION PLANS

Think about where you want to go on your next vacation. Consider your budget, the time of year, weather conditions, and the type of things you like to do. You can look for inspiration around you, such as exotic foods if you're in a supermarket, or perhaps posters or magazines being displayed inside a department store.

Be Inspired

Look for a food item you've never tried in someone else's cart. Find a recipe using it, then next time you do your shopping buy it and try it at home.

Put the Alphabet to Work

Try to write a pangram, from the Greek for "every letter," which is a sentence that uses every letter of the alphabet at least once. A classic example is:

"The quick brown fox jumps over the lazy dog."

Q: Why do restaurants and banks have customers wait in only one line?

A: Studies show that people in line are calmer if they have the same opportunity to reach their destination as everyone else. A single line is more equitable than several lines whose lengths vary unpredictably. Supermarkets don't use them because managing a snaking line of carts is too daunting.

A NEW USE FOR THE HUMBLE **SLEEVE**

You'll earn the gratitude of your children's teachers and the mothers of their friends if you take a few minutes to teach your kids proper sneeze and cough etiquette—sneezing or coughing into the sleeve! Make sure they understand that when they cough or sneeze, they are broadcasting germs that can make others sick.

The U.S. Centers for Disease Control and Prevention and the American Academy of Pediatrics both promote the concept of coughing into the upper sleeve (with arm raised and crooked around the face) rather than the hand as the best way to prevent the spread of germs sprayed by sudden-onset coughs and sneezes. Their point is that those who cover their faces with their hands most often proceed to spread the germs to doorknobs, phones, and whatever else gets touched.

While a disposable tissue is not a concept to be sneezed at, the reality is that children are not likely to always have a tissue ready. And they are also unlikely to run off to the nearest sink for a thorough hand washing every time they cough or sneeze, especially if they are stuck with you waiting in line. The sleeve technique, if it becomes a reflex, is a reasonable alternative.

. . . .

Lug Less While in Line

Standing in line is a good time to note if your purse, briefcase, or carryall weighs too much. Orthopedists recommend that the bags you carry often weigh no more than 10 percent of your body weight. So if you weigh 140 pounds (63.5 kg), your bag needs to be no more than 14 pounds (6.35 kg). Here are some facts to ponder:

- When choosing a carryall, look at the straps—the wider they are, the more evenly they will distribute the weight.

- Frequently switch your shoulder bag from one shoulder to the other to help reduce the stress.

- Teardrop-shape backpacks that center the weight close to the torso are the best option.

Kegel Exercise

This exercise tones the pubococcygeus muscle, a muscle found in both sexes that stretches from the pubic bone to the tailbone. Keeping this muscle strong can stave off urinary incontinence, help prevent prolapsed pelvic organs (common in women postchildbirth), and according to some, increase the ability to feel sexual pleasure. These exercises can be done anywhere without others noticing that you are doing them! Simply locate the muscles that you use to interrupt your flow of urine. Tighten those muscles and hold for a count of 10, and then relax for 10. Repeat 10 times.

IN LINE AND **STANDING PROUD**

While standing in line consider your posture. Is it a little slumped over? Bad posture can lead to poor digestion, inefficient circulation, and a decrease the amount of oxygen that you take in with each breath. The National Institutes of Health states that poor posture is a primary cause of back and neck problems. If you are standing in line near a wall, use it to discreetly assess your stance.

1. **Stand so that your head, shoulder blades, and backside touch the wall, with your heels 2–4 inches (5–10 cm) away from it.**

2. **Try to snugly slip your flattened hand between the wall and the "small," or curve, of your lower back.**

3. **If there is more than a hand's width of space, tighten your abdominal muscles to decrease the lumbar curve. If there is no room for your hand, lift your shoulders and increase the arch of your back.**

SOME SNEAKY, SUBTLE **STRETCHES**

While you're standing in line, you can unkink any muscles that are feeling cramped. Moderate stretching feels good when you've been inactive for a long time. Here are some traditional low-key stretches you can do without attracting too much attention from any nearby security guards!

Upper Body Stretches
Shrug your shoulders high and drop them. Rotate your shoulders in clockwise and counterclockwise circles. Clasp your hands behind your back. Slowly bring your arms up. Lean your upper body slightly forward as you lift your arms.

Chest Stretch
Let your arms fall open wide. Pull your arms back, squeezing your shoulder blades together. Depending on the size of your chest and the tightness of your garments, this may not be subtle!

Upper Back Stretch
While standing, clasp your hands out in front of you with straight arms and press out, rounding your upper back.

Shoulder Stretch
Grab your left forearm with your right hand and pull it across your chest, pressing it toward your body. Repeat on the other side.

Ankle Stretch
Make circles with your feet or trace the alphabet with your toes.

Quadriceps Stretch
If you don't mind a few stares, here's one for the quadriceps muscle at the front of the thigh. To steady yourself, grasp a stationary object (the pole of a rope divider marking out a line may not be steady enough). Use your other hand to clasp your ankle, and lift it behind you toward your backside. Keep your back straight and don't let the bending knee swing forward of the straight leg.

In Line

CHAPTER SIX

Outside

Whether you're waiting for a bus, walking around your yard, or breaking out your bicycle, being in the great outdoors has plenty to offer—even if you have only five minutes to enjoy it. Why not try some of the solutions in this chapter to help make the most of your time?

Outside Your House

If you have a few minutes to fill, turn your attention to your house's exterior. Here are some suggestions:

- Check your outdoor lights to see if any bulbs need replacing.
- Sweep your porch or steps.
- Hose off any plastic chairs; sweep off a wooden table.
- Clean up your woodpile; if it is covered by a tarp, make sure the tarp is being held down securely.
- If you have a fence, check it for weak spots or gaps.
- Inspect your lawn for stones, sticks, and any debris that can damage the lawn mower.
- Brush leaves off the bushes.

....

DRYER VENT CHECK

Check the vent-pipe outlet where your clothes dryer exhaust exits the house (typically a metal tube), and make sure it is not clogged by lint. If it is, use a brush or your hands to remove it. This simple check is crucial, because clogged dryer exhausts are a fire hazard. Outdoor vents should be covered by a hood with a flap to prevent small animals from entering the house through the vent.

....

"Home is where the heart is."

—Pliny the Elder
Roman scholar (A.D. 23–79)

FOUNDATION CHECK

You won't be able to do a really professional inspection of your home's foundation, but you can walk around the entire exterior of the house to check the side walls for cracks. Also look for cinder blocks that have shifted out of place, and check areas where brick meets the ground, looking for gaps between them.

If you do a check after it has rained, look for areas where water may have collected instead of draining away. Standing water like this may indicate that you need to have the ground around your house graded. Also check exterior windowsills for cracks, which may suggest that the ground beneath your foundation is sinking. If you note any areas of concern, call an expert for a professional evaluation. Many companies will do an initial evaluation for free.

Help Your Windshield

Clean out any leaf and stick debris that has collected in the well of your car windshield—where the wipers lie—the debris can interrupt the action of the wipers.

. . . .

Avoid Stings

Check around the eaves and ledges of your house for wasp, bee, or hornet nests that need to be removed. If you notice areas where a lot of wasps congregate around the eaves, you might want to spray those areas with insecticide. Otherwise, the wasps may enter your home during fall and hibernate over the winter, only to reemerge inside when the weather becomes warm!

. . . .

PREPARE FOR ICE WITH GRIPPY GRAVEL

If it's winter, put a bucket of sand near your front steps, garage door, or walkway for quick traction touch-ups on icy days. Sand is a reasonably effective source of traction and it is not toxic to pets, gardens, or groundwater, unlike rock salt and chemical deicers. You can also use cat litter in a pinch. If you prefer a deicer instead of just traction, the Center for Watershed Protection suggests using one with calcium magnesium acetate, which is less toxic than most deicers.

Outside

157

Here I Am

Take a few minutes to make sure it is easy for the fire department, ambulance, or other emergency responders to find you. Approach your house as if it's your first visit. If your address is not clearly visible from the road on a mailbox, signpost, or door of your home, now is the time to add it in adhesive reflective letters to one of these places, so that time is not lost finding your home in an emergency.

SHINY **MAILBOX**

If you've previously bought a package of adhesive reflectors, you can add a few to your mailbox to prevent cars from colliding with it on a dark night. However, instead of red reflectors, many town and highway safety department officials recommend using either blue or amber reflectors. This is because red reflectors can easily confuse tired drivers, who may try to follow the lights or brake suddenly to avoid them in the mistaken impression that they are a car or bicycle.

A BACKYARD **RESCUE OPERATION**

If you have children who play in the yard, there is a strong likelihood that your lawn is littered with miscellaneous toys, trucks mired in mud, and pieces of outdoor games, such as balls, bats, jump ropes, and racquets. To avoid making several trips, arm yourself with a laundry basket or large bag, and walk through the yard looking for the lost and abandoned. Of course, you might also be surprised to come upon your garden trowel.

Pet Owner Duty

If you have dogs with yard privileges, now might be a good time to police the yard with a pooper-scooper. If you have cats, look for their feces in the flower borders. You can use a small plastic bag to dispose of the feces—with your hand in the bag, grasp the feces with the bag, and then turn the bag inside out and deposit it in the trash.

COIL YOUR **GARDEN HOSE**

If your garden hose is lying in a heap in your yard, coil it neatly. Start where the hose connects to the faucet and work your way along the hose. Form the first loop, lay it on the ground, and move along the hose, unkinking it, and then lay the second loop on top of the first. Repeat until the entire hose is coiled.

In hot weather the hose will be reasonably compliant, but in cold weather you will be wrestling with a stiff, stubborn beast. Hoses used in the cold need to be drained after every use and stored indoors to make them easier to use and less prone to cracking. Outdoor storage in hot weather also poses risks if you use a polyvinyl chloride (PVC) hose, because heat increases the rate at which chemicals from the hose leach into the water. Any water in the hose expands in the heat, weakening the hose.

· ·

Q: Is water from a garden hose safe to drink?

A: Not necessarily, and it may not even be good for filling a child's wading pool. Many hoses are made from polyvinyl chloride (PVC), which contains lead used as a stabilizer. Especially in hot weather, when hoses are heated by the sun, lead can leach into the water. Brass hose fittings can also contain lead. In California, all hoses carry a warning, "This product contains chemicals known to the state of California to cause cancer, birth defects and/or reproductive harm." Drink-safe hoses are sold; these are often white or beige with a blue stripe and are labeled as safe to provide drinking water.

· ·

"Nothing is softer or more flexible than water, yet nothing can resist it." —Lao Tzu
Chinese philosopher (600–531 B.C.)

Outside

Fading Roses

To deadhead a rose, cut off the bloom at an angle above an outward-facing leaf bud for a hybrid tea rose. But remove the whole cluster back to the first leaf bud for a floribunda.

Deadhead Your Plants

The act of deadheading plants has nothing to do with dressing them in tie-dyed T-shirts. Instead, it is a method of interfering with the plant's natural processes, so that it will keep on blooming. Normally, a plant that blossoms, is fertilized, and sets (produces) seed has finished a complete reproductive cycle. The plant uses up its energy to set seed and will not bloom again in the current season. In fact, "go to seed" has become a metaphor for a person who is worn out and past his or her prime. Deadheading tricks the plant into beginning the flowering cycle again in the current season.

Deadheading, where the blossom is removed from the plant before it sets seed, does not hurt plants—to the contrary, it increases their vigor. To deadhead, snap (with your fingers) or snip (with pruning shears) off the plant's fading flowers. Not all plants will produce new blossoms if they are deadheaded (lilacs won't), but others, such as cosmos, marigolds, and zinnias, will bloom all season. Here are some others that will bloom again after deadheading:

- **Annuals** Most, including geraniums, pansies, snapdragons, verbena, nasturtiums, petunias, and pinks

- **Perennials** Bleeding heart, coral bells, coreopsis, delphiniums, Shasta and marguerite daisies, Russian sage, salvia, veronica, and sweet peas

. . . .

"All my possessions for a moment of time."
—Elizabeth I
Queen of England (1533–1603)

PREPARE FOR A **KITCHEN GARDEN**

In the fall, you can start to transform a small grassy area into a kitchen garden. Cover the selected lawn area with a thick layer of newspaper, then spread over some mulch, such as shredded leaves or bark, and water thoroughly. In the spring, the grass will have suffocated, and you won't have to do the hard work of sod-busting for your plot.

....

Rehome Some Earthworms

Go to a part of your yard that has loose, rich soil. Any damp place near woods or trees, fallen leaves, or a compost pile will be good. Use a small spade to dig for earthworms. If you find them, lift them gently with the spade and rehome them in a garden plot. The best natural soil conditioner are a few earthworms—they break up the soil, which lets oxygen in.

....

FORK OVER YOUR **COMPOST PILE**

If you have a compost pile, it only takes five minutes to turn it over with a garden fork or pitchfork. Forking over the pile and spreading the composting material around will allow oxygen into the pile, which is essential for proper composting. The word "compost" comes from the Latin words for "mixture" and "to put together," and by mixing with your fork and adding oxygen, you will speed the process of decomposition. There is also another benefit to turning the compost pile—it prevents it from becoming smelly.

....

Aerate Your Garden

You can aerate a garden by doing some light raking, and if yours is small, it will only take a few minutes. Raking aerates the soil under your garden, breaking up compacted soil and allowing crucial oxygen and water to penetrate to the roots of plants.

Outside

Collect Your Rainwater

Whether they live in the house or garden, all plants love rainwater, which is "soft" water—it has a lower concentration of calcium, lime, and magnesium salts than tap water—and it is also highly oxygenated. Ancient civilizations in arid countries, such as Jordan, devised elaborate cisterns for collecting precious rainwater. However, you can set up a simple system in five minutes by taking a large, clean plastic tub or even an old, enamel-lined soup pot and setting it out to catch the rain. In arid regions, you can go a step further by setting up a rain barrel—although this will take more than five minutes.

HARVEST A **CROP OF STONES**

If you live in a locale with stony soil, spend a few minutes collecting the stones from your garden, and piling them into a heap. Many places in North America, including Wisconsin, Michigan, Iowa, and New England, were once covered by glaciers, and today the land is covered by glacial till, or the stony sediments left behind as the glaciers receded. New England is crisscrossed by miles of stone walls, and the joke is that stones are the most reliable crop. In fact, it is frost heave—when the soil freezes and expands, and then thaws and contracts—that constantly pushes rocks up from the soil, giving the impression that the rocks have grown.

Participate in an ancient tradition by piling your rocks into a cairn, or stone heap. Cairns have marked sites of battle, slaughter, and burial; they are placed as welcome "this way" markers in the wilderness, and they are simply heaps— testimony to the hard labor of field clearing.

Death by Salad Dressing

Kill weeds that sprout up between walkway flagstones by pouring vinegar on them. Vinegar is acidic—and weeds will just pucker up and die.

No Illusions, Just Clouds

In popular tradition, clouds were viewed as the abode of the gods. Scientifically, however, clouds are specifically categorized by meteorologists. Clouds form when sunlight evaporates water from the earth's surface—the moisture-laden air rises and condenses around small particles of debris in the upper atmosphere to form clouds. Mountains can force moist air upward, which is why there are often clouds near them. Clouds absorb, scatter, and emit solar radiation, and they have major effects on the flow of energy in the earth's atmosphere.

In 1803 Luke Howard, an English naturalist, developed a cloud classification system based on labels derived from Latin. Clouds are also classified by base height—the prefix "cirro" means high, "alto" is middle, and "strato" or "stratus" means low. The next time you study the clouds for shapes, try to identify the basic cloud types—which might also help you determine if it will rain:

- **Cirrus** Latin for "curl of hair," a wispy cloud—known popularly as mares' tails. These form high in the atmosphere, where it turns into ice crystals—there is not enough moisture to cause rain.

- **Stratus** Latin for "layer," a sheetlike cloud. Rain can fall from this type of cloud, usually as a steady drizzle for a long period.

- **Cumulus** Latin for "heap," a puffy cloud—the favored cloud type for divine residences. These can be seen in any part of the atmosphere.

- **Nimbus** Latin for "violent rain," a rain cloud.

- **Cumulonimbus** These are cumulus clouds that are dark at their bases, but they can stretch high up the atmosphere. Rain can form in any part of the cloud but it doesn't necessarily reach the ground—this type of rain is known as virga. If you see dark cumulonimbus clouds, expect thunderstorms.

- **Altostratus/Altocumulus** If these gray midlevel clouds appear on a warm day, rain may follow.

Outside

Place Bird Alerts on Your Windows

When modern architects design buildings with vast expanses of glass panes, they probably intend to bring people closer to nature by bringing the outdoors indoors. Unfortunately, glass is a deceptive barrier for birds. They often don't see it, with the tragic result that they crash into the glass. Ornithologists estimate that over one billion birds a year are killed by colliding with glass. The problem is not well known because the bodies are often grabbed by scavengers, such as cats and gulls.

If you have large windows in your home, it takes only a few minutes to make them easier for birds to spot. Try these avian warnings:

- Place colorful streamers or wind chimes in front of the glass.

- Tape a hawk silhouette—available from ornithological societies or yard-supply stores—to the window.

- Attach stained-glass ornaments with suction cups to the windows.

- Place bird feeders near the windows. The birds will slow down for the feeder, so that they do not fly into the window.

. . . .

FATTEN UP **THE BIRDS**

The lives of birds are fraught with peril, from hazardous migration journeys to neighborhood cats. Make your yard one place they can look forward to a little TLC. Quick avian treats that you probably have in your pantry include peanut butter (smear it inside the hollowed-out peel of an orange half and hang it from a branch), sunflower seeds, dried cranberries, bread crumbs, crushed cornflakes, cornmeal, whole peanuts, chopped apples, and raisins. Put them out in an old, shallow baking pan. Leave out another pan full of water nearby.

Interpret the Flight of Birds

Imagine if politicians consulted birds—specifically, their flight patterns—rather than lobbyists when making public policy! In ancient Rome that is exactly what happened. Augurs interpreted bird flight patterns to guide the government. The Romans believed that the gods signaled their will via the patterns that a bird made in flight.

Today, it might be unwise to base your next stock purchase on the flight of a hawk, but can tell a lot about the bird you are observing from a quick analysis of its flight pattern. Here are some hints:

- **Soaring circle** Buteos (red-tailed hawk, red-shouldered hawk, common buzzard) use thermals, or updrafts of air caused by uneven heating near the earth's surface, to help overcome the air's resistance to their mass, enabling them to soar without flapping their wings. They soar in a circle to follow the path of the thermal.

- **Straight line** Accipiters (goshawks, Cooper's hawk, sharp-shinned hawk) fly in a straight line, flapping for several wing beats, and then glide on the momentum they've built up.

- **Strong wing beat** Falcons (prairie falcon, merlin, peregrine falcon) have strong wing beats; they seem to have places to go, and they rarely hover.

- **Crows and ravens** The practical crow flies in a straight line with even wing beats; the trickster raven plays about, alternating straight-ahead flapping with devil-may-care soaring.

- **Finches and woodpeckers** These both have undulating flight patterns, but finches veer up and down in steep rises and drops, while the woodpecker has a more gently rolling pattern.

Outside

A, My Name Is Alice...

Revisit your glory days on the playground and jump rope—and burn some calories at the same time! Just five minutes of jumping rope is equal to a ½-mile (800-m) run, according to the American College of Sports Medicine. Throw on your sneakers, and choose a level surface with a bit of give, such as a grassy lawn.

While you're exercising your heart, see if you can work your brain as well by trying to recall some of those traditional playground jump-roping rhymes that you once knew so well. Some rhymes date from the seventeenth century. Here's a popular rhyme to jog your memory:

Not last night but the night before
24 robbers came knocking at my door!
Call for the doctor, call for the nurse,
Call for the lady with the alligator purse.
In came the doctor, in came the nurse,
In came the lady with the alligator purse!

. . . .

Q: Do modern children have less free time?

A: Yes. A study conducted by the Survey Research Center at the University of Michigan found that from 1981 to 1997, children's free time each week decreased by approximately 12 hours—a 25 percent drop. Unstructured outdoor activity fell by 50 percent.

. . . .

"Life's tragedy is that we get old too soon and wise too late."

—Benjamin Franklin
American statesman (1706–90)

Tai Chi for the Family

Learning the Chinese martial discipline of tai chi is a life-long study, but you can put a few of its basic principles into practice within five minutes. This is a low-impact exercise suitable for every age group, so you can include the kids, too. The goal of tai chi is relaxed yet controlled power achieved through mindful, fluid movements. Tai chi teaches that by not expending your entire physical capacity you can free your body, mind, and spirit to tap into your inner source of life energy—your chi.

Here is a basic tai chi exercise:

1. Stand with your feet about 2 feet (60 cm) apart, facing forward, but not stiffly. Imagine that your head is being gently pulled upward from the crown, as though you were being held by a puppet string.

2. Tuck your chin slightly, and gaze forward with a soft gaze (not intensely focused on a particular point).

3. Relax your shoulders and let your arms hang loosely, with fingers apart in a slight, natural curl. Your palms need to face in toward your body.

4. Keep your knees relaxed, slightly bent, and your rear end slightly tucked in.

5. Bring your hands together with middle fingertips touching at a level about 2 inches (5 cm) below your navel. Your palms will now face upward as if you are making an offering.

6. Raise your hands in a slow, controlled movement to chest level, with fingertips still touching and palms up in offering. Breathe in and raise your body as you raise your hands.

7. Breathe out, and lower (slightly sink) your body as you return your hands to below your navel again, turning your palms to face the ground.

8. Repeat 6–8 times. Focus on the regular, controlled breathing in concert with the raising and lowering movements of your body and hands.

Improving Your Posture

Many people stand with most of their weight on one leg, or they slouch, placing stress on their joints and muscles. Even outdoors, you can work on your posture:

1. Stand with your feet slightly apart and knees straight, but not locked. Keep your head erect. Imagine there is a string from the top of your head giving you a lifted feeling through your spine.

2. Open your chest by keeping your shoulders relaxed, with shoulder blades down and back—do not arch your back. Keep your arms relaxed by your sides.

3. Keep your pelvis in a neutral position—rock your pelvis back and forth to find a comfortable place.

4. Feel your abdominal muscles being used, with a lifted feeling coming up and out of the hips. Keep your ribs and upper body balanced over your hips.

5. Now practice standing with your feet hips' distance apart, with your weight balanced over them. Check your feet to be sure they are not rolling in or out.

. . . .

Hold Your Tummy

To exercise your abdominal muscles outdoors, find a comfortable bench and follow these steps:

1. Sit on the bench so that your buttocks and back are as far away from the bench back as possible. Hold your abdominal muscles tight throughout the movement, and imagine a cord pulling up through the spine, keeping you as tall as possible.

2. Inhale as you slowly lean your torso and shoulders backward—keeping your spine rigid from hips to the top of the head—as far back as you feel comfortable.

3. Hold the pose for a moment, and exhale as you return to the first position. Do a set of 45 seconds; build up to 1–3 minutes per set for one to three sets.

TLC for Your Two-Wheeled Steed

If you're one of the many green-minded commuters who save money—it costs about two cents a mile to ride a bike—and the environment by commuting by bicycle, you can do one of these short-term bicycle checks and maintenance in five minutes. Of course, if you regularly ride your bicycle in traffic, you will want to do more extensive maintenance on a regular basis.

- **Tires** Use a pressure gauge to ensure that the tires are inflated to the recommended pressure printed on the side of the tire. Skinny tires may require air on a daily basis. If you're without a gauge, push the tire down hard on a paved surface. If it flattens, it needs air. Examine the tire for uneven wear, any glass or sharp gravel embedded in the tire, bulges, bubbles, or cuts.

- **Brake pads** Be sure that the ridges on the brake pads are not worn down. Check that the pads contact the rim of the tire, but not the tire itself or the spokes. Remove any dirt built up on the pads with a rag or old toothbrush.

- **Hand brakes** When you apply the hand brakes, there needs to be at least 1 inch (2.5 cm) of travel between the bar and the lever.

- **Chain** Maintaining the chain will extend the life of your bike's drivetrain. Remove dirt from the chain by turning the bike upside down, and then turn the pedal while you run a lint-free cloth along the chain. You can use an old toothbrush dipped in dish detergent to remove caked-on dirt.

- **Handlebars** Hold the front tire firmly between your legs (don't try this if you're wearing nice clothes) and try to turn the handlebars. If they turn, they are loose. Tighten the stem bolt.

Outside

Waiting for a Train (or Bus)

Waiting for a train or bus can seem like being in limbo—you just never know when the next one is about to show up. Here are a few suggestions to help pass the time:

- Check out what others are reading. If they seem really engrossed and the book or magazine seems like something you might like, make a note of it.

- Do an informal eyesight and hearing test. See how far away you can move before you can no longer read someone else's newspaper or hear a conversation.

- Imagine that you are taking a photograph and look around you to frame interesting images. If you have a camera on your cell phone, take a photo!

- If you're at a big city bus or subway stop, see how many famous or historical events you can think of that are associated with that locale.

- If you're waiting in a bus or subway station with a posted map of the transit system, study it so that you can become an expert navigator of your city.

- Write a silly note or a postcard (if you have one) to a friend, or send a text message in the style of old-fashioned vacation postcards: "Greetings from 29th Street! Having a great time! Wish you were here."

....

Q: Do cigarette butts eventually decompose?

A: Yes, but only after 12 years or more. Over 5.2 trillion cigarettes are produced yearly, but at least one in three end up as litter. Cigarette butts are made of cellulose acetate, which leaches toxic chemicals, including arsenic, cadmium, and lead, as they decompose. Butts pollute the water supply when they are washed into streams and sewers and have been found inside fish. You'll be helping the environment by stopping to pick up butts in your spare minutes.

Text Message like a Teenager

If you're of a certain age and struggling to text messages, these shortcuts may be a revelation—and what better time to practice than while waiting for a train or bus:

BBFN	Bye-bye for now	**IMHO**	In my humble opinion
B/C	Because		
BION	Believe it or not	**IOU1**	I owe you one
BRB	Be right back	**JAM**	Just a minute
BRT	Be right there	**LMHO**	Laughing my head off
CMIW	Correct me if I'm wrong		
		LOL	Laugh out loud
EML	E-mail me later	**NRN**	No reply necessary
GIGO	Garbage in garbage out	**RUOK**	Are you OK?
		SWL	Screaming with laughter
GMTA	Great minds think alike		
		TTYL	Talk to you later
GTG	Got to go	**WFM**	Works for me

....

Name That Column

Three basic styles of column developed by the ancient Greeks are still omnipresent in today's buildings. Spend some spare minutes studying the architectural details on the buildings in your vicinity.

- **Doric** Has a simple, cylindrical shaft without a base, topped by a circle surmounted by a square (known as the capital).

- **Ionic** Taller than the Doric, it is fluted (grooved), with a stack of rings for the base. The capital is adorned with scrolls, or volutes.

- **Corinthian** Like the Ionic, but the capital is adorned with botanical forms, often acanthus leaves.

Outside

INDEX

PHOTO CREDITS

Dave Klug: Cover, 8, 20, 28, 37, 43, 49, 54, 65, 66, 72, 82, 85, 97, 103, 112, 119, 122, 124, 128, 134, 142, 144, 146, 154, 156, 164, 171

Viv Foster: 17, 32

Shutterstock: All chapter icons and icons on running feet, 26, 56, 71, 131

ACKNOWLEDGMENTS

TOUCAN BOOKS
Project Designer Viv Foster
Project Editor Theresa Bebbington
Managing Editor Ellen Dupont
Proofreader Marion Dent
Indexer Michael Dent

Toucan Books would like to thank Susan Clarke, MCSP, member of the chartered society of physiotherapy, for her assistance in many of the exercise solutions.